DIVINE MOMENTS FOR STUDENTS

Everyday Inspiration from God's Word

DIVINE MOMENTS

MOMENTS

for

STUDENTS

Everyday Inspiration

from God's Word

Tyndale House Publishers, Inc.

Carol Stream, Illinois

Visit Tyndale's exciting Web site at www.tyndale.com

TYNDALE, New Living Translation, NLT, and the New Living Translation logo are registered trademarks of Tyndale House Publishers, Inc.

Divine Moments for Students: Everyday Inspiration from God's Word

Questions and notes copyright © 2008 by Ronald A. Beers. All rights reserved.

Cover photo copyright © by Photodisc. All rights reserved.

Managing editors: Ronald A. Beers and Amy E. Mason

Contributing writers: V. Gilbert Beers, Rebecca J. Beers, Brian R. Coffey, Jonathan Farrar, Jeffrey Frasier, Jonathan Gray, Shawn A. Harrison, Sandy Hull, Rhonda K. O'Brien, Douglas J. Rumford, Linda Taylor

Designed by Julie Chen

Edited by Michal Needham

Scripture quotations are taken from the *Holy Bible,* New Living Translation, copyright © 1996, 2004. Used by permission of Tyndale House Publishers, Inc., Carol Stream, Illinois 60188. All rights reserved.

ISBN-13: 978-1-4143-1228-6

ISBN-10: 1-4143-1228-8

Printed in the United States of America

14   13   12   11   10   09   08

7   6   5   4   3   2   1

Introduction

The goal of *Divine Moments for Students* is to help you experience a breakthrough with God, to show you how and where God is at work in your life to get your attention each day. If the Bible is really a blueprint for living, then God, through his Word, should be able to respond to any question you have for him. And he does! As you read the questions and Scripture in this book, it is amazing to see how God's answers to your daily needs are so clear and help you see with "spiritual eyes" how he is trying to break through to you. Sometimes God seems so big and mysterious that you may wonder whether he would truly bother with you. But he loves you personally and is trying to get your attention every day. This little book can help you notice the divine moments when he is trying to show you how much he cares. You can read straight through the book, or you can use it topically when you are looking for God's help in a certain area of life or if you just need more clarity about what God might say about something that is important to you. We pray this little book will be meaningful to you and help you experience many divine moments with God.

—The editors

Abilities

How can I make the most of my abilities?

A Moment *with* God

It is not that we think we are qualified to do anything on our own. Our qualification comes from God.

2 Corinthians 3:5

My life is worth nothing to me unless I use it for finishing the work assigned me by the Lord Jesus.

Acts 20:24

I brought glory to you here on earth by completing the work you gave me to do.

John 17:4

What gives you the right to make such a judgment? What do you have that God hasn't given you? And if everything you have is from God, why boast as though it were not a gift?

1 Corinthians 4:7

God gives all people special abilities and spiritual gifts that he intends them to develop and use. Do you know what yours are? One of the most important tasks in life is to identify your unique abilities and gifts. Then you have three choices: First, you could ignore them. This will leave you unfulfilled and disconnected from God's plan for you. Second, you could use them to advance your own goals because you are naturally gifted in certain areas. Third, you could put them to their intended use and maximize God's purpose for you. As you read and obey God's Word, you will begin to understand your special abilities and spiritual gifts. Taking a spiritual-gifts assessment would also help. Once you know what they are, using your unique abilities and gifts to serve God will give you deep satisfaction and help you discover your distinct role among God's people.

DIVINE PROMISE

TO THOSE WHO USE WELL WHAT THEY ARE GIVEN, EVEN MORE WILL BE GIVEN, AND THEY WILL HAVE AN ABUNDANCE.   *Matthew 25:29*

Absolutes

MY QUESTIONS *for* GOD

Are there absolutes in life? How can I know what they are?

A MOMENT *with* GOD

People may be right in their own eyes, but the LORD examines their heart.   PROVERBS 21:2

In those days Israel had no king; all the people did whatever seemed right in their own eyes.   JUDGES 21:25

Your job is to obey the law, not to judge whether it applies to you.   JAMES 4:11

*I*magine you've just bought a new cell phone or computer. If you ignore the instructions for using it, it will still work. But you'll miss out on so many of the great things it was meant to do; you'll miss out on so much of what you could have enjoyed. Now let's say that instead of ignoring the instructions, you go against them—you purposely do the opposite of what the manual tells you to do. Suddenly you've got a bigger problem. Your phone or computer will only frustrate you because nothing is working right. There's a certain way to get these gadgets to work, and the instruction book tells you how. It's the same with life. The Bible is God's instruction manual for living. When you follow his instructions, life just works better. That's because God, as the creator of life, has programmed certain absolutes into the world—principles that apply to all people in all times and all places. Ignore God's instructions, and you'll miss out on so much of what God intends for you to enjoy in life. Go against his instructions, and life isn't going to work at all. You will be hurt, frustrated, and disappointed. That's why it is so important to read the Bible and discover what always works and what never works. Then life will be so much smoother, more enjoyable, and more fulfilling.

Divine Promise

ALL SCRIPTURE IS INSPIRED BY GOD AND IS
USEFUL TO TEACH US WHAT IS TRUE AND TO
MAKE US REALIZE WHAT IS WRONG IN OUR
LIVES. IT CORRECTS US WHEN WE ARE WRONG
AND TEACHES US TO DO WHAT IS RIGHT.

2 Timothy 3:16

Acceptance

MY QUESTION *for* GOD

Can God help me accept other people?

A MOMENT *with* GOD

Accept each other just as Christ has accepted you so
that God will be given glory.   ROMANS 15:7

Accepting others is the key to good relationships.
Without it, you would likely lead a life of rejection and
loneliness. But accepting others and feeling accepted
by them allows you to develop friendships. God accepts you no matter what—despite the times you've
hurt him, ignored him, or rejected him. Only when
you understand God's unconditional love will you be
drawn into a relationship with him. God calls you to
accept others in the same way that he does because
he knows how important it is to have deep friendships
and how much influence you can have in the lives of
others. Just as God accepted you for who you are and
then challenged you to grow and change, so you must
accept others for who they are before you try to influence them. Acceptance isn't about befriending the best
or most godly people. Acceptance is about letting God
break through your fears, inhibitions, and stereotypes
in order to bring out the best in the people around you.
God also calls you to accept those the world deems unacceptable—the poor, the homeless, the handicapped,
the elderly, prisoners, and addicts.

DIVINE PROMISE

THOSE THE FATHER HAS GIVEN ME WILL COME
TO ME, AND I WILL NEVER REJECT THEM.
John 6:37

Accomplishments

MY QUESTION *for* GOD

How can I know if my accomplishments are pleasing God?

A MOMENT *with* GOD

After his baptism, as Jesus came up out of the water,
the heavens were opened and he saw the Spirit of God
descending like a dove and settling on him. And a
voice from heaven said, "This is my dearly loved Son,
who brings me great joy." MATTHEW 3:16-17

This Good News tells us how God makes us right in
his sight. This is accomplished from start to finish by
faith. As the Scriptures say, "It is through faith that a
righteous person has life." ROMANS 1:17

You didn't choose me. I chose you. I appointed you to
go and produce lasting fruit, so that the Father will
give you whatever you ask for, using my name.

JOHN 15:16

We are God's masterpiece. He has created us anew in
Christ Jesus, so we can do the good things he planned
for us long ago. EPHESIANS 2:10

*M*any people assume that accomplishing great things is the way to become spiritually great. They are driven to earn respect from others, to impress others, to gain the applause and approval of others. If you are striving for these things, it can easily transfer over to your relationship with God—you may think you have to earn his love and forgiveness too. But you are accepted because of God's grace, not because of what you accomplish. God accepted you from the start, before you had accomplished anything. It's true that you have been created, called, and equipped to accomplish certain things for God. But your accomplishments are always to be understood as the result of God's grace in you, not your own efforts. The greatest accomplishment is allowing God to carry out his plans through you. This means letting go of your need to be accepted because of your performance. God-pleasing accomplishments will highlight God's power at work in you.

DIVINE PROMISE

WITH GOD'S HELP WE WILL DO
MIGHTY THINGS.   *Psalm 60:12*

Accountability

MY QUESTION *for* GOD

How can accountability deepen my relationship with God?

A MOMENT *with* GOD

"Can anyone hide from me in a secret place? Am I not everywhere in all the heavens and earth?" says the LORD.   JEREMIAH 23:24

You must commit yourselves wholeheartedly to these commands that I am giving you today. Repeat them again and again to your children. Talk about them when you are at home and when you are on the road, when you are going to bed and when you are getting up. Tie them to your hands and wear them on your forehead as reminders. Write them on the doorposts of your house and on your gates. . . . Do what is right and good in the LORD's sight, so all will go well with you.   DEUTERONOMY 6:6-9, 18

Accountability is literally giving an account of yourself—where you've been, what you've been doing, what your motives were. The one who is holding you accountable has the freedom to ask for this account from you. The purpose of accountability is not to keep you from having fun but to help you enjoy life even more by preventing you from impulsively doing something that will hurt yourself or someone else. With the right person holding you accountable, you will make better decisions that will positively impact your future. You may not always like to be held accountable; you may think it puts too many restrictions on you. It forces you to open up the dark corners of your life that you'd prefer to keep hidden. But accountability will keep you honest, happy, and on the right path. It's not always

comfortable, but it's necessary. Ultimately, accountability means answering to God. If you're really going
to take it seriously, you have to begin with God as your
primary accountability partner. He knows all the secrets of your heart anyway, so why try to hide anything
from him? Be honest with God, and tell him about your
struggles. Follow his principles for living as found in
the Bible. Then you'll be less likely to do something
you will later regret. You will better understand what
you are doing and why you are doing it when you understand for whom you are doing it.

DIVINE PROMISE
YOU WILL ALWAYS HARVEST WHAT YOU PLANT.
Galatians 6:7

Addiction

MY QUESTION *for* GOD
How can God break the power of addiction in my life?

A MOMENT *with* GOD
You say, "I am allowed to do anything"—but not
everything is good for you. And even though "I am
allowed to do anything," I must not become a slave
to anything.   1 CORINTHIANS 6:12

Don't copy the behavior and customs of this world,
but let God transform you into a new person by

changing the way you think. Then you will learn to know God's will for you, which is good and pleasing and perfect.   ROMANS 12:2

You belong to God, my dear children. You have already won a victory . . . because the Spirit who lives in you is greater than the spirit who lives in the world.   1 JOHN 4:4

The Holy Spirit produces this kind of fruit in our lives: love, joy, peace, patience, kindness, goodness, faithfulness, gentleness, and self-control.

GALATIANS 5:22-23

*W*ho in their right mind would volunteer to become a slave, chained forever to a life of bondage? That's exactly what addiction is: self-imposed slavery. It's selling yourself into a lifetime of bondage to a habit or substance. While we often think of addiction as a problem related to drugs or alcohol, there are other addictions that are just as destructive. You can become addicted to laziness, watching television, playing computer games, eating unhealthy food—the list goes on and on. You can even become addicted to good things, like exercising too much or eating too much health food. We all have our addictions, whether they are simply bad habits or serious dependencies. Sin is the worst addiction. Like other addictive habits or substances, sin often appears alluring and attractive and promises short-term pleasure. You can easily justify giving in just this once, thinking you have things under control. But soon you realize that your "one time" has turned into a habit you can't stop. It now controls you. As with other addictions, sin often results when you lose self-control. Ironically, the only way to recover your self-control is to let God control you. His control is always for your benefit and for your spiritual growth. God can break the power of any addiction you are struggling with when you give him control of your life. It is imperative that you admit your addiction and acknowledge its destructiveness. God often works through other people to help you. It is almost impossible to overcome addiction by yourself; you need the consistent support of people who love you enough to tell you the truth and hold you accountable. But you must also hold yourself accountable to God's way of living, as written in the Bible. This will keep you close to God, and he will work in your life to change your heart and desires. Surrender to the Holy Spirit, and God will replace addictive impulses with life-affirming desires. While it is important to seek the help of others, it is only with God's help that you will ultimately have the power to overcome addiction.

DIVINE PROMISE

YOU ARE NOT CONTROLLED BY YOUR SINFUL NATURE. YOU ARE CONTROLLED BY THE SPIRIT IF YOU HAVE THE SPIRIT OF GOD LIVING IN YOU. *Romans 8:9*

Advice

I'm bombarded with opinions. How do I know whether I'm getting the right advice?

The LORD says, "I will guide you along the best pathway for your life. I will advise you and watch over you."   PSALM 32:8

If you need wisdom, ask our generous God, and he will give it to you. He will not rebuke you for asking.

JAMES 1:5

Then Jehoshaphat added, "But first let's find out what the LORD says."   1 KINGS 22:5

What should I do? This is a commonly asked question. In an age of conflicting claims and confusing information, many people are searching for wise counsel. Maybe that's why counselors are in such great demand and advice columnists are in every newspaper. But there's a critical difference between well-meaning advice and wise counsel. God's wisdom is best because he is all-knowing. Seek knowledge and understanding from the One who knows everything that will happen today and tomorrow and every day to come. Then you will have the wisdom to weigh and interpret advice from others.

Let the message about Christ, in all its richness, fill
your lives. Teach and counsel each other with all the
wisdom he gives.   COLOSSIANS 3:16

The word of God is alive and powerful. It is sharper
than the sharpest two-edged sword, cutting between
soul and spirit, between joint and marrow. It exposes
our innermost thoughts and desires.   HEBREWS 4:12

All Scripture is inspired by God and is useful to teach
us what is true and to make us realize what is wrong
in our lives. It corrects us when we are wrong and
teaches us to do what is right.   2 TIMOTHY 3:16

*B*e careful if a friend or adviser always seems to be
telling you what you want to hear. It may be a sign that
he or she is more interested in gaining your favor than
building your faith. The Word of God is described as
sharp because it cuts all the way down to your motives. Good advisers won't always tell you what you
want to hear because sometimes they will need to use
God's Word to convict you of sin. Divine moments often come unexpectedly through convicting yet timely
words of advice!

DIVINE PROMISE
YOU GUIDE ME WITH YOUR COUNSEL, LEADING
ME TO A GLORIOUS DESTINY.   *Psalm 73:24*

Anger

MY QUESTION *for* GOD

Why do I get so angry sometimes?

A MOMENT *with* GOD

The LORD accepted Abel and his gift, but he did not accept Cain and his gift. This made Cain very angry, and he looked dejected. GENESIS 4:4-5

"You have made me look like a fool!" Balaam shouted. NUMBERS 22:29

"Didn't I tell you?" the king of Israel exclaimed to Jehoshaphat. "He never prophesies anything but trouble for me. . . . Put this man in prison, and feed him nothing but bread and water!" 1 KINGS 22:18, 27

"Get out of the sanctuary, for you have sinned."
. . . Uzziah, who was holding an incense burner, became furious. 2 CHRONICLES 26:18-19

When Haman saw that Mordecai would not bow down or show him respect, he was filled with rage.
ESTHER 3:5

Anger is often a reaction to your pride being hurt. When you are confronted, rejected, ignored, or don't get your way, anger acts as a defense mechanism to protect your ego. It is common to feel angry when someone confronts you about your own sinful actions because you don't want others to know that you've done something wrong. When anger begins to well up inside you, stop and ask yourself, *Who is really offended in this situation? Is this about God's honor or my pride? Am I acting out of humility or revenge?* Confession, forgiveness, and reconciliation will melt your anger away.

DIVINE PROMISE
A GENTLE ANSWER DEFLECTS ANGER, BUT HARSH WORDS MAKE TEMPERS FLARE.
Proverbs 15:1

Anticipation

MY QUESTION *for* GOD
How can I learn to anticipate the great things God has planned for me?

A MOMENT *with* GOD

When the Lamb broke the seventh seal on the scroll, there was silence throughout heaven for about half an hour.   REVELATION 8:1

Now we live with great expectation, and we have a priceless inheritance—an inheritance that is kept in heaven for you, pure and undefiled, beyond the reach of change and decay. And through your faith, God is protecting you by his power until you receive this salvation, which is ready to be revealed on the last day for all to see. So be truly glad. There is wonderful joy

ahead, even though you have to endure many trials
for a little while.   1 PETER 1:3-6

You guide me with your counsel, leading me to a
glorious destiny.   PSALM 73:24

Think of what heaven will sound like—reverberating
with joyful shouts and songs of ceaseless praise. Now
imagine heaven becoming perfectly quiet, as it does
when the seventh seal is opened in Revelation. You've
probably experienced, in a moment of tension or fear,
how just a few seconds of silence can seem to last a
lifetime—heaven is quiet for half an hour! Only something very important could cause this silence. What
is it? The awe of anticipation. Like the hush in a the-
ater when the houselights are dimmed and the curtain
starts to rise, millions of heaven's residents become silent when they realize something momentous is about
to happen. Our lives are noisy too—but, sadly, they
resound more often with ringing phones and droning
televisions than with the praise and worship of God.
Do you ever pause and wonder what momentous things
God might be preparing to do next in your life? How
many divine moments of awe-inspiring anticipation do
you miss by never being still before God? Discipline
yourself to build a few moments of silent anticipation
into each day, making time to pray and open yourself
up to what God wants to do in and through you. It
is in these moments with God that he will reveal just
enough of his plan to make you ready for his great purposes in your life. Come before him with reverent awe

and anticipation for the glorious future that lies ahead
of you.

DIVINE PROMISE

"I KNOW THE PLANS I HAVE FOR YOU," SAYS THE
LORD. "THEY ARE PLANS FOR GOOD AND NOT
FOR DISASTER, TO GIVE YOU A FUTURE AND
A HOPE." *Jeremiah 29:11*

Apathy

MY QUESTIONS *for* GOD

*How am I supposed to get excited about God? What if I just
don't care?*

A MOMENT *with* GOD

I know all the things you do, that you are neither hot
nor cold. I wish that you were one or the other! But
since you are like lukewarm water, neither hot nor
cold, I will spit you out of my mouth!

REVELATION 3:15-16

Don't just pretend to love others. Really love them.
Hate what is wrong. Hold tightly to what is good.

ROMANS 12:9

Anyone who isn't with me opposes me, and anyone
who isn't working with me is actually working
against me.   MATTHEW 12:30

Watch out! Don't let your hearts be dulled by
carousing and drunkenness, and by the worries
of this life. Don't let that day catch you unaware.

LUKE 21:34

In the book of Revelation, apathy is compared to lukewarm water. Cold water quenches thirst and refreshes
a parched mouth. Hot water is used for cooking and
sanitizing. But lukewarm water has little value. Apathy
is much the same. When apathy settles in, passion and
purpose are gone. Apathy is like a parasite that feeds on
your motivation and devours your talents and gifts. One
of Satan's greatest lies is that following God and doing his
work are nothing to be excited about. That couldn't be
farther from the truth! It is only through following God
and getting involved in serving him that your life will
have meaning, energy, and purpose. In fact, the supernatural Spirit of God is a driving force within you, lighting a passion for service in your heart and encouraging
purpose rather than boredom. God's Word describes the
antidote to apathy: purposeful work, a thankful heart,
and serving others. These three things can help you fight
off feelings of apathy, renew your focus on God's purpose for your life, and anticipate with excitement the
blessings God has in store for you.

DIVINE PROMISE

GOD IS NOT UNJUST. HE WILL NOT FORGET
HOW HARD YOU HAVE WORKED FOR HIM AND
HOW YOU HAVE SHOWN YOUR LOVE TO HIM

BY CARING FOR OTHER BELIEVERS, AS YOU
STILL DO. OUR GREAT DESIRE IS THAT YOU
WILL KEEP ON LOVING OTHERS AS LONG AS
LIFE LASTS, IN ORDER TO MAKE CERTAIN THAT
WHAT YOU HOPE FOR WILL COME TRUE. THEN
YOU WILL NOT BECOME SPIRITUALLY DULL
AND INDIFFERENT.   *Hebrews 6:10-12*

Apology

MY QUESTION *for* GOD

*Is it really that important to apologize when I've done
something wrong?*

A MOMENT *with* GOD

The high and lofty one who lives in eternity, the Holy
One, says this: "I live in the high and holy place with
those whose spirits are contrite and humble. I restore
the crushed spirit of the humble and revive the
courage of those with repentant hearts."   ISAIAH 57:15

Confess your sins to each other and pray for each
other so that you may be healed.   JAMES 5:16

His son said to him, "Father, I have sinned against
both heaven and you, and I am no longer worthy
of being called your son." But his father said to the
servants, "Quick! Bring the finest robe in the house
and put it on him. . . . for this son of mine was dead
and has now returned to life. He was lost, but now
he is found."   LUKE 15:21-24

Saying "I'm sorry" for something you have done wrong is one of the most difficult things to do. You have to admit your fault, face it head-on, and then humble yourself enough to confess it to someone else. A sincere apology is the first step in changing your behavior and committing to do the right thing from now on. Refusing to apologize when you know you're wrong is a sign of pride, which can have devastating effects on your life and relationships. But being willing to apologize demonstrates humility and opens the door to healing and blessing. If you need a breakthrough in your relationship with a friend, a classmate, or God himself, the practice of apologizing when you are wrong will help you reach a new level of trust and respect. Lasting change can only take place in a humble heart. When you can admit your faults and ask for forgiveness, you will experience a divine moment in which God begins to heal your heart and relationships. Is it time for you to apologize to God or someone else?

DIVINE PROMISE

PEOPLE WHO CONCEAL THEIR SINS WILL NOT PROSPER, BUT IF THEY CONFESS AND TURN FROM THEM, THEY WILL RECEIVE MERCY. BLESSED ARE THOSE WHO FEAR TO DO WRONG, BUT THE STUBBORN ARE HEADED FOR SERIOUS TROUBLE. *Proverbs 28:13-14*

Appearance

MY QUESTION for GOD

How can I see beyond appearances?

A MOMENT with GOD

Charm is deceptive, and beauty does not last.

PROVERBS 31:30

Don't be concerned about the outward beauty of
fancy hairstyles, expensive jewelry, or beautiful
clothes. You should clothe yourselves instead with
the beauty that comes from within, the unfading
beauty of a gentle and quiet spirit, which is so
precious to God.   1 PETER 3:3-4

If you listen to the word and don't obey, it is like
glancing at your face in a mirror. You see yourself,
walk away, and forget what you look like.   JAMES 1:23-24

Appearance does matter—just make sure you're
looking at the right things. Your body, face, and clothes
reflect only your outward shell, which is in a constant
process of aging and decay. Your soul and character reflect your inner being, which is ageless and eternal and
shows who you really are. There's nothing wrong with
paying attention to your physical appearance, but not
to the neglect of your spiritual appearance. Walking
with God causes you to reflect his beauty. Let God's
perfect character be reflected from within you, and let
your true appearance shine.

DIVINE PROMISE

PEOPLE JUDGE BY OUTWARD APPEARANCE, BUT
THE LORD LOOKS AT THE HEART.   *1 Samuel 16:7*

Approval

MY QUESTION *for* GOD

*I work so hard to please others. What do I have to do to gain
God's approval?*

A MOMENT *with* GOD

When I tried to keep the law, it condemned me.

GALATIANS 2:19

There is only one God, and he makes people right
with himself only by faith, whether they are Jews
or Gentiles.   ROMANS 3:30

Nothing in all creation will ever be able to separate us
from the love of God that is revealed in Christ Jesus
our Lord.   ROMANS 8:39

What causes us to approve of some people and not
others? Too often it comes down to appearance or performance. You don't like the way someone looks, or
you don't like something they've done. Or perhaps the
shoe's on the other foot, and you find it hard to win the
approval of someone else. In one sense, it's entirely appropriate for your boss or your teachers to disapprove

of your work if you are not meeting their standards of performance. It's also entirely appropriate for God to disapprove of your behavior if you are enjoying a lifestyle that is contrary to his commandments. But there's another kind of approval that everyone needs, and it should never be based on performance. It is the unconditional love we all long for. In a good family you find love and acceptance no matter how you look or what you do. This is a picture of what it's like to be in God's family. As a child of God, created in his image, God loves and accepts you not for what you do but for who you are. The fact that God created you gives you great worth. He loves you and approves of you because you are his, no matter what you think about him or what others think about you. The knowledge that nothing you can do will cause God to love you any less should motivate you to do all you can to please him.

DIVINE PROMISE

THE KINGDOM OF GOD IS NOT A MATTER OF WHAT WE EAT OR DRINK, BUT OF LIVING A LIFE OF GOODNESS AND PEACE AND JOY IN THE HOLY SPIRIT. IF YOU SERVE CHRIST WITH THIS ATTITUDE, YOU WILL PLEASE GOD, AND OTHERS WILL APPROVE OF YOU, TOO.   *Romans 14:17-18*

Arts

How can I experience God through the arts?

A MOMENT *with* GOD

Beautiful words stir my heart. I will recite a lovely
poem about the king, for my tongue is like the pen
of a skillful poet.   PSALM 45:1

He cared for them with a true heart and led them
with skillful hands.   PSALM 78:72

Send me a master craftsman who can work with
gold, silver, bronze, and iron, as well as with purple,
scarlet, and blue cloth. He must be a skilled engraver
who can work with the craftsmen of Judah and
Jerusalem who were selected by my father, David.

2 CHRONICLES 2:7

And now, son of man, take a large clay brick and set it
down in front of you. Then draw a map of the city of
Jerusalem on it. Show the city under siege. . . . This
will be a warning to the people of Israel.   EZEKIEL 4:1-3

Sing a new song of praise to him; play skillfully on
the harp, and sing with joy.   PSALM 33:3

Creativity is built into every human being. God made
you creative so that you could express yourself in ar-
tistic ways—through worshiping, singing, loving,
helping, playing music, crafting beautiful objects, or

thinking through problems. There is an expressive beauty in the arts that can create powerful emotions. But each expression of your creativity needs to be God-honoring because creativity is a characteristic of God. When presented appropriately, the arts can be powerful mediums for helping others experience God. For example, God inspired Jeremiah to draw a sketch of Jerusalem under siege in order to warn the people about God's displeasure over their sinful lifestyle and to move them to repentance. The arts can be misused, however, and thus they also have the potential to turn people away from God. You must stay away from either creating or enjoying art that tempts you toward sinful desires. With your specific creative talents, you have a responsibility to reflect God's creative image in appropriate ways. Have you ever been moved by the worshipful overtures of a song or the heavenly lighting captured in a beautiful painting? Perhaps the emotions you experience through the arts are divine moments in which your expressive and creative God is touching your heart in new ways.

DIVINE PROMISE

WE ARE GOD'S MASTERPIECE. HE HAS CREATED US ANEW IN CHRIST JESUS, SO WE CAN DO THE GOOD THINGS HE PLANNED FOR US LONG AGO. *Ephesians 2:10*

Ashamed

MY QUESTION *for* GOD

Why do I sometimes feel ashamed about sharing my faith?

A MOMENT *with* GOD

If anyone is ashamed of me and my message in these adulterous and sinful days, the Son of Man will be ashamed of that person when he returns. MARK 8:38

When you are ridiculed for your faith, it is natural to feel embarrassed because it is natural to want to fit in with others. But if you remember that faith is a life-and-death matter, it can give you the strength to not only stand up for what you believe but to share the Good News with others. People may become curious about your faith when they see how seriously you take the promises of God. They may even come to realize their own need for him.

I am not ashamed of this Good News about Christ.

ROMANS 1:16

Paul was not ashamed of the Good News because he knew that only the gospel holds the power to save souls for eternity. Those who know Jesus truly know the secret to living forever. Rather than embarrass you, this should empower you.

Never be ashamed to tell others about our Lord.

2 TIMOTHY 1:8

*I*t is difficult to share your faith with others if you think you will be ridiculed for it. But the Bible doesn't say you need to go out on a street corner and shout it out. Instead, you should be prepared to explain to others why you live the way you do. Your loving actions toward them should compel them to wonder how you came to be this way. You have nothing to be ashamed of because you are merely showing them God's love.

DIVINE PROMISE

BE HAPPY WHEN YOU ARE INSULTED FOR BEING A CHRISTIAN, FOR THEN THE GLORIOUS SPIRIT OF GOD RESTS UPON YOU.   *1 Peter 4:14*

Awesome

MY QUESTIONS *for* GOD

Why is it important to recognize the awesomeness of God? What happens in me when I see it?

A MOMENT *with* GOD

Who is like you among the gods, O LORD—glorious in holiness, awesome in splendor, performing great wonders?

EXODUS 15:11

Who can comprehend the power of your anger?
Your wrath is as awesome as the fear you deserve.

PSALM 90:11

Everyone was gripped with great wonder and awe,
and they praised God, exclaiming, "We have seen
amazing things today!"   LUKE 5:26

God's awesome power is captivating, but fearing God
is different from fearing other powerful things. You
take cover from the power of a severe storm or run
from the power of a crashing wave on the shore. Yet
being in awe of God's power draws you toward him
rather than away from him. The more you see God's
awesomeness at work in your life and in the world
around you, the more you will want to be near him and
experience his empowering Spirit. Recognizing God's
awesomeness puts you in the middle of his glory. Being
in awe of God helps you experience his presence and
unconditional love.

DIVINE PROMISE

I HAVE HEARD ALL ABOUT YOU, LORD.
I AM FILLED WITH AWE BY YOUR AMAZING
WORKS. IN THIS TIME OF OUR DEEP
NEED, HELP US AGAIN AS YOU DID IN
YEARS GONE BY. AND IN YOUR ANGER,
REMEMBER YOUR MERCY. *Habakkuk 3:2*

Balance

MY QUESTION *for* GOD

How can maintaining balance in my life help me better experience God?

A MOMENT *with* GOD

As soon as Jesus heard the news, he left in a boat to a remote area to be alone. But the crowds heard where he was headed and followed on foot from many towns. Jesus saw the huge crowd as he stepped from the boat, and he had compassion on them and healed their sick.   MATTHEW 14:13-14

Jesus often withdrew to the wilderness for prayer.

LUKE 5:16

One day soon afterward Jesus went up on a mountain to pray, and he prayed to God all night. At daybreak he called together all of his disciples and chose twelve of them to be apostles.   LUKE 6:12-13

It's tempting to think that God is most pleased by constant service. Yet Jesus modeled a life of balance between socializing and solitude, action and reflection, mission and meditation. He worked hard to help others, and then he took time for spiritual renewal. This pace allowed him to remain open to God's direction instead of being driven by human pressures. Balance is about keeping the right pace in life—not moving so fast that you miss God's call, but not moving so slow that you miss the opportunities God sends you. Balance helps you realize that not every opportunity is the call of God. It leaves you open to divine moments and motivates you to act on them.

DIVINE PROMISE

YOU SEE ME WHEN I TRAVEL AND WHEN I REST AT HOME. YOU KNOW EVERYTHING I DO.
Psalm 139:3

Beginnings

MY QUESTION *for* GOD

How can I begin again and get a fresh start without the burdens of the past?

A MOMENT *with* GOD

Create in me a clean heart, O God. Renew a loyal spirit within me.   PSALM 51:10

Put on your new nature, created to be like God—truly righteous and holy.   EPHESIANS 4:24

Great is his faithfulness; his mercies begin afresh each morning.   LAMENTATIONS 3:23

People dream of new beginnings—an escape from sameness, a chance to wipe the slate clean and start over, an opportunity to move away from past hurts, or maybe just a chance to do something different. For some people a new beginning is threatening because it forces them away from what is known and comfortable. For others it is exciting—a challenge to move into new territory, or the exhilaration of an unknown adventure. Life is actually a series of new beginnings. You can't avoid change. It's not a matter of whether change will come but how you will deal with it when it does. You are probably more accustomed to new beginnings than you think, for each day brings new challenges and problems. Each day also brings new opportunities to get to know God better and to start over with a new attitude toward circumstances and people. Because God renews his mercies to you every single day, you don't have to be burdened by yesterday's failures or regrets. So embrace the dawn of each new day as a divine moment, a chance to start again and to experience the refreshing mercies of God.

DIVINE PROMISE

I AM CERTAIN THAT GOD, WHO BEGAN THE GOOD WORK WITHIN YOU, WILL CONTINUE HIS WORK UNTIL IT IS FINALLY FINISHED ON THE DAY WHEN CHRIST JESUS RETURNS.

Philippians 1:6

Belonging

MY QUESTION *for* GOD

What does it mean to belong to God?

A MOMENT *with* GOD

If you obey the commands of the LORD your God
and walk in his ways, the LORD will establish you as
his holy people as he swore he would do. Then all the
nations of the world will see that you are a people
claimed by the LORD, and they will stand in awe
of you.   DEUTERONOMY 28:9-10

Such people claim they know God, but they deny him
by the way they live.   TITUS 1:16

If you love me, obey my commandments.   JOHN 14:15

*M*oses spent a great deal of time reciting all the
blessings that would come to the Israelites if they were
faithful in obeying God. Obedience is an important part
of belonging to God because it shows others that you
love him. It is out of love that God gives his commands
to his people, in order to protect and guide them and to
ensure that they experience life to the fullest. Obeying
God is a sign that you have accepted God's call to be
in relationship with him and that you belong to him.
Disobeying God is not so much about breaking a law
as breaking God's heart by showing that you don't love
him. God is your heavenly Father, who welcomes you
into his family and showers you with blessings as you

obey him. These blessings may not always be material
things, but they are always rich and satisfying—such
as peace of mind, lasting joy, and being in God's presence. Belonging to God is about the daily experience
of a satisfying relationship with him and sharing in the
blessings that come from belonging to his family.

DIVINE PROMISE

KEEP THE WAY OF THE LORD BY DOING WHAT IS
RIGHT AND JUST. THEN I WILL DO . . . ALL THAT
I HAVE PROMISED.   *Genesis 18:19*

Best

MY QUESTION *for* GOD

Why should I give my best to God?

A MOMENT *with* GOD

"Should people cheat God? Yet you have cheated
me! But you ask, 'What do you mean? When did we
ever cheat you?' You have cheated me of the tithes
and offerings due to me. You are under a curse, for
your whole nation has been cheating me. Bring all
the tithes into the storehouse so there will be enough
food in my Temple. If you do," says the LORD of
Heaven's Armies, "I will open the windows of heaven
for you. I will pour out a blessing so great you won't
have enough room to take it in! Try it! Put me to
the test!"

MALACHI 3:8-10

In all that he did in the service of the Temple of God and in his efforts to follow God's laws and commands, Hezekiah sought his God wholeheartedly. As a result, he was very successful.   2 CHRONICLES 31:21

The people answered with one voice, "We will do everything the LORD has commanded."   EXODUS 24:3

Giving your best to God shows the value you put on your relationship with him. If you are trying to get away with less than your best, your motives reveal that God is not first in your life. Giving God only what is leftover of your income shows that you value money more than God. Spending time with God only when it's convenient for you shows that you value your own schedule more than time with him. Since what you value reflects the condition of your heart, giving your best to God reflects what you think of him. And giving less than your best cheapens God's best gifts to you—salvation and eternal life through the death and resurrection of his own Son, Jesus. While it may seem like an overwhelming task to always give your best for God, it is actually the very thing that energizes you. When you give to God first from your income, you are blessed with excitement as you see how it helps others. When you give God your time to serve others, you are blessed with peace in your relationships. When you give your best to God, he showers you with divine blessings!

DIVINE PROMISE

WORK WILLINGLY AT WHATEVER YOU DO, AS
THOUGH YOU WERE WORKING FOR THE LORD
RATHER THAN FOR PEOPLE. REMEMBER THAT
THE LORD WILL GIVE YOU AN INHERITANCE AS
YOUR REWARD, AND THAT THE MASTER YOU
ARE SERVING IS CHRIST.   *Colossians 3:23-24*

Bible

MY QUESTION *for* GOD

How does God speak to me through the Bible?

A MOMENT *with* GOD

When I discovered your words, I devoured them.
They are my joy and my heart's delight, for I bear
your name, O LORD God of Heaven's Armies.

JEREMIAH 15:16

Your promise revives me; it comforts me in all
my troubles.   PSALM 119:50

Your laws please me; they give me wise advice.

PSALM 119:24

All Scripture is inspired by God and is useful to teach
us what is true and to make us realize what is wrong
in our lives. It corrects us when we are wrong and
teaches us to do what is right. God uses it to prepare
and equip his people to do every good work.

2 TIMOTHY 3:15-17

Some people miss out on the incredible experience of reading God's Word because they think it's boring, irrelevant, or too hard to live by. But daily Bible reading not only draws you closer to God, it is also a truly exciting adventure as you get a glimpse into the mind of God himself. If you're having trouble reading the Bible, start with smaller portions and take extra time to consider what you read. Try to imagine what it would have been like to live at the time the passage was written. Imagine yourself in the stories and events you read about. Use a Bible with study notes, or read a commentary along with the Scripture passage. Does the reading bring you hope or comfort? Is there a promise you can claim? Is there a life principle you can take to heart? These glimmers of hope, comfort, guidance, and wisdom are the ways in which God touches your heart. The miracle of the Bible is that it is living—it has general truths that apply to all people in all times and places, but it also speaks specifically to your life and current situation. God has written the Bible to everyone as well as to you individually. Think of reading the Bible as a journey of discovery to see what God is saying to you.

Divine Promise

I WILL PUT MY LAWS IN THEIR MINDS, AND I WILL WRITE THEM ON THEIR HEARTS. I WILL BE THEIR GOD, AND THEY WILL BE MY PEOPLE.

Hebrews 8:10

Boredom

MY QUESTION for GOD

How should I deal with boredom?

A MOMENT with GOD

As a door swings back and forth on its hinges, so the
lazy person turns over in bed.   PROVERBS 26:14

Let's not get tired of doing what is good. At just the
right time we will reap a harvest of blessing if we
don't give up.   GALATIANS 6:9

Imitate God, therefore, in everything you do. . . .
Live a life filled with love, following the example
of Christ.   EPHESIANS 5:1-2

The dictionary defines *boredom* as being weary with
tedious dullness. It might come from doing the same
thing over and over or doing work with no apparent
purpose or doing nothing for too long. Many people
with hectic schedules say, "I'd love to be bored for a
while." But there's a difference between boredom and
rest. Everyone needs rest, but no one needs boredom.
Boredom is dangerous because it signifies lack of purpose and passion for anything meaningful. The antidote to boredom is finding something purposeful and
significant to do. God has a purpose for you, and finding that purpose is a divine moment. From that time
on, you will never be bored! It may sound like a lot of
effort, but the more you search for meaning by serv-

ing God, the more divine moments you'll have as God energizes your spirit and guides you in the right direction. Start by volunteering in a ministry at your local church, or find a hobby that helps you develop a skill. Then you will have something to look forward to each day. Whatever you do, search for the things that make you feel God's pleasure—you'll never be bored.

DIVINE PROMISE

OUR GREAT DESIRE IS THAT YOU WILL KEEP ON LOVING OTHERS AS LONG AS LIFE LASTS, IN ORDER TO MAKE CERTAIN THAT WHAT YOU HOPE FOR WILL COME TRUE. THEN YOU WILL NOT BECOME SPIRITUALLY DULL AND INDIFFERENT.   *Hebrews 6:11-12*

Brokenness

MY QUESTIONS *for* GOD

What does it mean to be broken? How can brokenness strengthen me spiritually?

A MOMENT *with* GOD

[Job said to God,] "I take back everything I said, and I sit in dust and ashes to show my repentance."   JOB 42:6

The LORD is close to the brokenhearted; he rescues those whose spirits are crushed.   PSALM 34:18

The sacrifice you desire is a broken spirit. You will
not reject a broken and repentant heart, O God.

PSALM 51:17

All praise to God, the Father of our Lord Jesus
Christ. God is our merciful Father and the source of
all comfort. He comforts us in all our troubles so that
we can comfort others. When they are troubled, we
will be able to give them the same comfort God has
given us.   2 CORINTHIANS 1:3-4

*B*rokenness is the awareness of your full dependence
on God. It signifies the breaking of your pride and self-
sufficiency. Brokenness often comes through circumstances that overwhelm you or through sin that reduces
you to nothing. You realize that the only way out of
your mess is through God's help. Those who are open
about their brokenness are often influential in helping
others. If you have been broken, allow God to use your
experience to help others overcome their struggles.
And be encouraged. Through your brokenness, God is
expanding your capacity to obey and serve him.

DIVINE PROMISE

I WILL BLESS THOSE WHO HAVE HUMBLE
AND CONTRITE HEARTS, WHO TREMBLE AT
MY WORD.   *Isaiah 66:2*

Burnout

MY QUESTION *for* GOD

*I'm burning the candle at both ends. How do I find the
strength to keep going when it seems I have nothing left?*

A MOMENT *with* GOD

When David and his men were in the thick of battle,
David became weak and exhausted.   2 SAMUEL 21:15

I am exhausted and completely crushed. My groans
come from an anguished heart.   PSALM 38:8

Only in returning to me and resting in me will
you be saved. In quietness and confidence is your
strength.   ISAIAH 30:15

Come to me, all of you who are weary and carry
heavy burdens, and I will give you rest. . . . You will
find rest for your souls.   MATTHEW 11:28-29

He gives power to the weak and strength to the
powerless. Even youths will become weak and tired,
and young men will fall in exhaustion. But those who
trust in the LORD will find new strength. They will
soar high on wings like eagles. They will run and not
grow weary. They will walk and not faint.

ISAIAH 40:29-31

Burnout is an overwhelming exhaustion and in-
ability to push on, usually brought about by too much
stress. We all experience times of burnout, when we

feel tapped out emotionally, mentally, physically, and spiritually. In our fast-paced, 24-7 world, it isn't surprising that we become quickly exhausted. Because burnout is so draining and paralyzing, you need to take care of your body and mind by eating right, exercising, and getting enough sleep and relaxation. Otherwise you won't be able to function effectively. One of the best ways to reduce burnout is to take time out to be close to God. If you're burning the candle at both ends, more than likely you are neglecting your time with God. When you draw close to him, you can tap into his power, strength, peace, protection, and love. Schedule some time to think about God's Word or read a book that challenges you spiritually. As you focus on God's priorities, your priorities will become clear.

DIVINE PROMISE

THE LORD IS MY SHEPHERD; I HAVE ALL THAT
I NEED. HE LETS ME REST IN GREEN MEADOWS;
HE LEADS ME BESIDE PEACEFUL STREAMS.
HE RENEWS MY STRENGTH. HE GUIDES ME
ALONG RIGHT PATHS, BRINGING HONOR
TO HIS NAME. *Psalm 23:1-3*

Busyness

MY QUESTION *for* GOD

I'm constantly rushing around, but when I rest, I feel like I'm wasting time. How can I learn to enjoy both work and leisure?

A Moment *with* God

Enthusiasm without knowledge is no good; haste
makes mistakes.   PROVERBS 19:2

Plant your seed in the morning and keep busy all
afternoon, for you don't know if profit will come
from one activity or another—or maybe both.

ECCLESIASTES 11:6

He lets me rest in green meadows; he leads me beside
peaceful streams.   PSALM 23:2

We often operate under the false assumption that being busy means being productive and that resting means
being lazy. But it's possible to have unproductive activity and productive rest! There are many benefits of being busy, such as earning a living, meeting deadlines at
work or school, and advancing God's Kingdom by serving those in need. But being too busy can damage your
relationships (with God and with others), cause burnout, or prevent you from focusing on your real priorities.
As with anything you do, learning to strike a balance
between working, serving, having fun, and resting will
allow you to be productive in all areas of life and will
give you many divine moments with God.

DIVINE PROMISE
TEACH US TO REALIZE THE BREVITY OF LIFE, SO
THAT WE MAY GROW IN WISDOM.   *Psalm 90:12*

Call of God

MY QUESTION *for* GOD

What is God calling me to do?

A MOMENT *with* GOD

My life is worth nothing to me unless I use it for
finishing the work assigned me by the Lord Jesus.

ACTS 20:24

God's gifts and his call can never be withdrawn.

ROMANS 11:29

Now may the God of peace—who brought up
from the dead our Lord Jesus, the great Shepherd
of the sheep, and ratified an eternal covenant with
his blood—may he equip you with all you need
for doing his will. May he produce in you, through
the power of Jesus Christ, every good thing that is
pleasing to him.   HEBREWS 13:20-21

*D*eep down inside, do you long to be a part of something bigger than yourself? Do you wonder why you
were born and what you should do with your life? This
is God calling you to discover the reason he created
you. Often people wish God's call would come in the
form of an audible voice or a miraculous sign in the sky.
The truth is, God doesn't always call people to extraor-
dinary, life-changing adventures like being a missionary in Africa—although sometimes he does. God's call
is often a task right in front of you, something you can

do today; it might be working in the nursery at your church, caring for an ailing professor, making dinner at a local soup kitchen, or volunteering at a homeless shelter. God has given you special gifts and abilities, and he wants you to use them now, not just five or ten years from now. When you use your abilities to serve God and other people, you are answering God's call. As you do, you will also be prepared when he calls you to something much bigger. In everything he calls you to do, you can be sure he will equip you with the desire, vision, support, and resources you need to carry it out.

DIVINE PROMISE

MAY THE GOD OF PEACE MAKE YOU HOLY IN
EVERY WAY, AND MAY YOUR WHOLE SPIRIT
AND SOUL AND BODY BE KEPT BLAMELESS
UNTIL OUR LORD JESUS CHRIST COMES AGAIN.
GOD WILL MAKE THIS HAPPEN, FOR HE WHO
CALLS YOU IS FAITHFUL.   *1 Thessalonians 5:23-24*

Challenges

MY QUESTIONS *for* GOD

What should I keep in mind when I face new challenges?
Where can I get the extra strength I need to overcome them?

A MOMENT *with* GOD

A prudent person foresees danger and takes
precautions. The simpleton goes blindly on and
suffers the consequences.   PROVERBS 22:3

Do not be afraid of the terrors of the night, nor the
arrow that flies in the day.   PSALM 91:5

Commit everything you do to the LORD. Trust him,
and he will help you.   PSALM 37:5

The LORD had said to Abram, "Leave your native
country, your relatives, and your father's family, and
go to the land that I will show you."   GENESIS 12:1

"Now go, for I am sending you to Pharaoh. You
must lead my people Israel out of Egypt." But Moses
protested to God, "Who am I to appear before
Pharaoh? Who am I to lead the people of Israel out
of Egypt?" . . . Then Moses and Aaron returned to
Egypt and called all the elders of Israel together.
Aaron told them everything the LORD had told
Moses, and Moses performed the miraculous signs
as they watched. Then the people of Israel were
convinced that the LORD had sent Moses and Aaron.
When they heard that the LORD was concerned about
them and had seen their misery, they bowed down
and worshiped.   EXODUS 3:10-11; 4:29-31

"The Israelites are confused. They are trapped in the
wilderness!" . . . Then Moses raised his hand over
the sea, and the LORD opened up a path through the
water with a strong east wind. The wind blew all that

night, turning the seabed into dry land. So the people of Israel walked through the middle of the sea on dry ground, with walls of water on each side!

EXODUS 14:3, 21-22

*T*hose who have great faith are risk takers who embrace the challenges of life. Abram left everyone and everything he knew when he responded to God's challenge to move to a new place. God told Moses to stand before Pharaoh and demand that he release the Israelites, and later God used him to part the Red Sea and lead the people through forty years of wilderness wanderings. Great things do not happen without challenges. In fact, great things don't happen until ordinary people respond to big challenges. The next time you are faced with a challenge, have faith that God is by your side and wants to help you overcome it. Step out boldly in obedience, and watch how God opens the way for you.

DIVINE PROMISE

IN YOUR STRENGTH I CAN CRUSH AN ARMY;
WITH MY GOD I CAN SCALE ANY WALL.

2 Samuel 22:30

Change

*With so many changes in my life, how can I keep it all
together?*

God our Father, who created all the lights in the
heavens . . . never changes or casts a shifting shadow.

JAMES 1:17

In his unfailing love, my God will stand with me.

PSALM 59:10

Jesus Christ is the same yesterday, today, and forever.

HEBREWS 13:8

If you need wisdom, ask our generous God, and he
will give it to you. He will not rebuke you for asking.

JAMES 1:5

The character of God is unchanging and thus completely reliable. This is good news because no matter
how much your life changes, no matter what new situations you face, God promises to go with you, to love
you, and to help you. He also promises to give you
wisdom to deal with change when you ask him for it.

Heaven and earth will disappear, but my words will
never disappear.   MARK 13:31

The truths and advice in the Bible apply to all people in all cultures in all times. This is important because the standards of living you find in the Bible always apply; you can always count on them to work for you, every single day. As you face change, constantly turn to God's unchanging Word to maintain your perspective and give your life a rock-solid foundation.

When the Ishmaelites, who were Midianite traders, came by, Joseph's brothers pulled him out of the cistern and sold him to them for twenty pieces of silver. . . . Then Pharaoh said to Joseph, " . . . You will be in charge of my court, and all my people will take orders from you. Only I, sitting on my throne, will have a rank higher than yours."

GENESIS 37:28; 41:39-40

We know that God causes everything to work together for the good of those who love God and are called according to his purpose for them.   ROMANS 8:28

Sometimes change seems to be for the worse. Joseph was sold by his own brothers into slavery, but through that terrible experience he became governor of all of Egypt. When change makes you feel like you're going to fall apart, remember that traumatic, unpredictable, and unfair change never trumps God's will. Nothing takes God by surprise. You can truly experience a divine moment when God takes a bad situation in your life and turns it into something wonderful.

DIVINE PROMISE
I AM THE LORD, AND I DO NOT CHANGE.
Malachi 3:6

Character

MY QUESTION *for* GOD

What does my character reveal about who I am?

A MOMENT *with* GOD

My prayer is not for the world, but for those you have given me, because they belong to you. All who are mine belong to you, and you have given them to me, so they bring me glory.   JOHN 17:9-10

You are a holy people, who belong to the LORD your God. Of all the people on earth, the LORD your God has chosen you to be his own special treasure.

DEUTERONOMY 7:6

The Holy Spirit produces this kind of fruit in our lives: love, joy, peace, patience, kindness, goodness, faithfulness, gentleness, and self-control.

GALATIANS 5:22-23

Those who are called God's people are special—holy, dedicated to him, and chosen to be his own. This is a special privilege, but it is also a great responsibility because it requires you to model the very character of God. In fact, your character is a means of revealing God's character to the world. Because God is always with you, you have the help you need to display the godly characteristics of love, joy, peace, patience, kindness, goodness, faithfulness, gentleness, and self-control. If you belong to God, your life should reveal his character in these ways. What kind of character does your life reveal?

DIVINE PROMISE

GOD BLESSES THOSE WHOSE HEARTS ARE PURE,
FOR THEY WILL SEE GOD. *Matthew 5:8*

Choices

MY QUESTION *for* GOD

How can I learn to make better choices?

A MOMENT *with* GOD

When Jesus came by, he looked up at Zacchaeus and called him by name. "Zacchaeus!" he said. "Quick, come down! I must be a guest in your home today." Zacchaeus quickly climbed down and took Jesus to his house in great excitement and joy. But the people were displeased. "He has gone to be the guest of a notorious sinner," they grumbled. Meanwhile, Zacchaeus stood before the Lord and said, "I will give half my wealth to the poor, Lord, and if I have

cheated people on their taxes, I will give them back
four times as much!"   LUKE 19:5-8

*Z*acchaeus had made some bad choices—the people
in the crowd called him a "notorious sinner." But after Jesus spent some time with him, Zacchaeus was
changed, and he wanted to make better choices. Your
choices reflect the kind of person you are, which is often influenced by the people you spend time with. The
more time you spend with someone, the more likely it
is that he or she will influence your decisions. In the
same way, when you spend time with Jesus, you'll find
yourself making choices that please him and avoiding
choices that don't. Zacchaeus began to change, in both
his behavior and his attitudes, when he spent time with
Jesus. The change in Zacchaeus started with his choice
to welcome an encounter with the transforming power
of God. That is the best choice you can make too!

DIVINE CHALLENGE
YOU CAN MAKE THIS CHOICE BY LOVING
THE LORD YOUR GOD, OBEYING HIM, AND
COMMITTING YOURSELF FIRMLY TO HIM.
Deuteronomy 30:20

Choices

How do I know if I've made the right choices?

A MOMENT *with* GOD

I appeal to you to show kindness to my child,
Onesimus. I became his father in the faith while here
in prison. Onesimus hasn't been of much use to you
in the past, but now he is very useful to both of us.
I am sending him back to you, and with him comes
my own heart. . . . He is no longer like a slave to you.
He is more than a slave, for he is a beloved brother.

PHILEMON 1:10-12, 16

*W*hy are the right choices often the hardest ones to
make? The verses above are about a slave named Onesimus who wronged his master in some way and then
ran away. While on the run, Onesimus met the apostle
Paul, who introduced him to Jesus. Onesimus's life was
changed, and he then had to choose to do the right thing
by returning to his master, Philemon. Philemon had
to choose to accept him back without punishing him
harshly. It would not be easy for Onesimus to return
to Philemon, and it would not be easy for Philemon to
take his slave back and accept him as a fellow believer.
Paul advised both men to make the right choice. When
you are making the right choice, God will confirm it
deep in your heart, and other people you trust will affirm it too. Knowing the right way doesn't always make

it easier to choose it, but knowing your choice is right can give you the courage to do what you need to do.

DIVINE CHALLENGE

WHAT YOU OUGHT TO SAY IS, "IF THE LORD WANTS US TO, WE WILL LIVE AND DO THIS OR THAT." OTHERWISE YOU ARE BOASTING ABOUT YOUR OWN PLANS, AND ALL SUCH BOASTING IS EVIL. REMEMBER, IT IS SIN TO KNOW WHAT YOU OUGHT TO DO AND THEN NOT DO IT.

James 4:15-17

Choices

MY QUESTION *for* GOD

How can I be certain I'm choosing God's ways?

A MOMENT *with* GOD

Love the LORD your God, walk in all his ways, obey his commands, hold firmly to him, and serve him with all your heart and all your soul.   JOSHUA 22:5

Choose today whom you will serve. . . . As for me and my family, we will serve the LORD.   JOSHUA 24:15

I have hidden your word in my heart, that I might not sin against you.   PSALM 119:11

There is safety in having many advisers.   PROVERBS 11:14

*E*ach day presents you with many choices. The best choices you can always make are to honor God and obey his Word. These decisions will always point you toward God's ways and put you squarely in the center of his will. To help you make good choices, read God's Word, seek his advice in prayer, and ask for help from godly friends and mentors. Avoid choices that benefit you at the expense of others. It may not be complicated, but it is challenging to put God before everything else in your life and to put others before yourself. Each day offers you the choice to serve the Lord; by following these guidelines and maintaining a "God first" attitude, you can know with certainty that you are choosing God's ways.

DIVINE PROMISE

HE GUIDES ME ALONG RIGHT PATHS, BRINGING
HONOR TO HIS NAME.   *Psalm 23:3*

Church

MY QUESTION *for* GOD

How can I experience God by going to church?

A MOMENT *with* GOD

The one thing I ask of the LORD—the thing I seek most—is to live in the house of the LORD all the days of my life, delighting in the LORD's perfections and meditating in his Temple.   PSALM 27:4

What joy for those who can live in your house, always
singing your praises.   PSALM 84:4

*E*ven though God lives in the heart of every believer,
he also lives within the community of the church.
When God's people are gathered together, they meet
God in a special way. Just as being present at a live
concert or sports event makes it much more exciting,
participating with other believers in worshiping God
makes it much more meaningful.

Just as our bodies have many parts and each part
has a special function, so it is with Christ's body.
We are many parts of one body, and we all belong
to each other.   ROMANS 12:4-5

*G*od has given all believers special gifts. Some are
great organizers and administrators while others are
gifted musicians, teachers, even dishwashers! When
everyone in a congregation uses their gifts to serve others, the church becomes a powerful force for good, a
strong witness for Jesus, and a mighty army to combat
Satan's attacks against God's people in your community. The church needs you because the body of Christ
is not complete without you!

Let us not neglect our meeting together, as some
people do, but encourage one another, especially
now that the day of his return is drawing near.

                                            HEBREWS 10:25

$\mathcal{G}$ood friends are a wonderful gift, and fellowship among believers is even more wonderful because the living God promises to be in their midst. The church brings together people who have a common perspective on life. Christian fellowship provides a place for honest sharing, for encouragement to stay strong in the face of temptation and persecution, and for godly wisdom to deal with problems.

DIVINE PROMISE

WHERE TWO OR THREE GATHER TOGETHER AS MY FOLLOWERS, I AM THERE AMONG THEM.
Matthew 18:20

$\mathcal{C}ommitment$

MY QUESTION *for* GOD

What does it mean to be committed to God?

A MOMENT *with* GOD

Jesus called out to them, "Come, follow me, and I will show you how to fish for people!" And they left their nets at once and followed him.   MATTHEW 4:19-20

Give your bodies to God.   ROMANS 12:1

$\mathcal{B}$eing committed to God requires a decision of the mind followed by an act of the will. Commitment wraps up your thoughts and actions into a common purpose. Commitment is more than intellectual agreement; it involves a sacrificial giving of the whole self.

If you do not carry your own cross and follow me, you cannot be my disciple. But don't begin until you count the cost.   LUKE 14:27-28

*B*eing committed to God can be costly. To follow him, you might have to leave other attractive things behind.

"If we are thrown into the blazing furnace, the God whom we serve is able to save us. . . . But even if he doesn't, we want to make it clear to you, Your Majesty, that we will never serve your gods or worship the gold statue you have set up." DANIEL 3:17-18

*B*eing committed to God is being willing to accept the sometimes painful consequences of obeying him. When you are committed to God, there will always be those who oppose you and everything you stand for. This is the essence of spiritual warfare, and as in any battle, there will be some wounds.

Trust in the LORD with all your heart; do not depend on your own understanding. Seek his will in all you do, and he will show you which path to take.

                                                    PROVERBS 3:5-6

*B*eing committed to God means that you trust him to lead you and do what is best for you. Without complete trust in God, you will be distracted by every doubt and selfish desire. Commitment allows you to trust God and endure even when you don't understand his ways.

DIVINE PROMISE

IF WE ARE FAITHFUL TO THE END, TRUSTING GOD JUST AS FIRMLY AS WHEN WE FIRST BELIEVED, WE WILL SHARE IN ALL THAT BELONGS TO CHRIST.   *Hebrews 3:14*

Communication

MY QUESTION *for* GOD

How do I know when God is speaking to me?

A MOMENT *with* GOD

My sheep listen to my voice; I know them, and they follow me.   JOHN 10:27

Anyone who belongs to God listens gladly to the words of God.   JOHN 8:47

*T*he best way to be certain you are hearing God's voice is to know God. If you don't know God, how can you recognize his voice?

Before daybreak the next morning, Jesus got up and
went out to an isolated place to pray.   MARK 1:35

Be still, and know that I am God! I will be honored
by every nation. I will be honored throughout the
world.   PSALM 46:10

*P*rayer is conversing with God and building a relationship with him. Good conversation always includes listening—allowing God to speak to you. Only when you
listen to God can he make his wisdom and resources
available to you. Sometimes it's good to spend time
with God without actually verbalizing your prayer. Just
meditate on God or his Word. Then listen and be ready
to hear him speak to your mind and heart. As you listen, you will learn to distinguish between your own
thoughts and the voice of God.

The word of God is alive and powerful. It is sharper
than the sharpest two-edged sword, cutting between
soul and spirit, between joint and marrow. It exposes
our innermost thoughts and desires.   HEBREWS 4:12

*J*ust as a piano is tuned against a standard tuning
fork, so you become in tune with God when you check
yourself against the standards for living found in the
Bible. As God communicates to you through the Bible,
you will begin to discern just what he wants you to do.
As your spiritual hearing improves, you will be able to
respond more readily when God calls you to a certain
task that he has reserved just for you.

Who can know the Lord's thoughts? Who knows
enough to teach him? But we understand these
things, for we have the mind of Christ.

1 CORINTHIANS 2:16

When you become a Christian, the Holy Spirit helps
you understand the mind of Christ. He gives guidance,
wisdom, and discernment that is not available to those
who don't know the Lord.

DIVINE PROMISE

DON'T WORRY ABOUT ANYTHING; INSTEAD,
PRAY ABOUT EVERYTHING. TELL GOD WHAT
YOU NEED, AND THANK HIM FOR ALL HE
HAS DONE. THEN YOU WILL EXPERIENCE
GOD'S PEACE. *Philippians 4:6-7*

Competition

MY QUESTION *for* GOD

How can I use my competitive nature in appropriate ways?

A MOMENT *with* GOD

"Come, let's build a great city for ourselves with a
tower that reaches into the sky. This will make us
famous and keep us from being scattered all over the
world." But the LORD . . . scattered them all over the
world, and they stopped building the city.

GENESIS 11:4-5, 8

*T*here's nothing wrong with having a competitive nature. However, that competitive drive can cause you
to focus too much on pursuing your own goals rather
than pursuing God's plans for you. Such self-centered
pursuits can tempt you to build your own tower of Ba-
bel, a monument to commemorate your own efforts.
But if you're not interested in what God wants you to
achieve, you'll never achieve anything of lasting value.
Ask God to help you channel your competitive nature
into the pursuit of accomplishments and actions that
will last for eternity.

Work willingly at whatever you do, as though you
were working for the Lord rather than for people.

COLOSSIANS 3:23

*Y*ou are called to work hard to do your best, not to
compete against others simply to beat them. If beating
others is your only goal, you honor only yourself. If
doing your best is your goal, you honor the God who
created you.

Thank God! He gives us victory over sin and death.

1 CORINTHIANS 15:54

*U*ltimately the greatest victory you can achieve in life
is eternal life through faith in God. If you keep your eye
on that goal, you will be able to handle lesser victories
or defeats with more grace. It is through humble hearts

that God accomplishes the greatest victories. That's something to strive for!

DIVINE PROMISE

WHATEVER I AM NOW, IT IS ALL BECAUSE GOD POURED OUT HIS SPECIAL FAVOR ON ME—AND NOT WITHOUT RESULTS. FOR I HAVE WORKED HARDER THAN ANY OF THE OTHER APOSTLES; YET IT WAS NOT I BUT GOD WHO WAS WORKING THROUGH ME BY HIS GRACE.
1 Corinthians 15:10

Compromise

MY QUESTION *for* GOD

How do I know when it's okay to compromise and when it's not?

A MOMENT *with* GOD

Make me truly happy by agreeing wholeheartedly with each other, loving one another, and working together with one mind and purpose.   PHILIPPIANS 2:2

If the godly give in to the wicked, it's like polluting a fountain or muddying a spring.   PROVERBS 25:26

Dear friend, don't let this bad example influence you. Follow only what is good.   3 JOHN 1:11

You will be successful if you carefully obey the decrees and regulations that the LORD gave to Israel

through Moses. Be strong and courageous; do not be
afraid or lose heart!   1 CHRONICLES 22:13

I want my way, you want yours, and neither one of
us is going to give in." This is a familiar story, whether
it's played out at home, at school, at work, or in any
relationship. Compromise is the art of negotiating so
that both sides win. When it is a time to compromise,
each side should give a little so that both sides gain
something and a greater good is accomplished. However, there are times when you should not compromise.
When the forces of evil tempt you to sin, you must not
give in. To compromise God's truth, God's ways, or
God's Word is to negotiate with that which is unholy.
The test of acceptable compromise is simple: Can you
reach an agreement that satisfies both parties without
sacrificing anyone's morals? If you give up godliness in
exchange for anything else, it's a bad bargain. Your goal
should be to choose God's ways above your own at all
costs. That's always a win-win situation!

DIVINE CHALLENGE

YOU MUST ALWAYS ACT IN THE FEAR OF
THE LORD, WITH FAITHFULNESS AND AN
UNDIVIDED HEART.   *2 Chronicles 19:9*

Conscience

My Question *for* God

How does God use my conscience to guide me?

A Moment *with* God

They know the truth about God because he has made it obvious to them. For ever since the world was created, people have seen the earth and sky. Through everything God made, they can clearly see his invisible qualities—his eternal power and divine nature. So they have no excuse for not knowing God.

Romans 1:19-20

Cling to your faith in Christ, and keep your conscience clear. For some people have deliberately violated their consciences; as a result, their faith has been shipwrecked.

1 Timothy 1:19

I have the same hope in God . . . that he will raise both the righteous and the unrighteous. Because of this, I always try to maintain a clear conscience before God and all people.

Acts 24:15-16

Your conscience is the inner part of you that helps you know if you are doing right or wrong, if you are obeying God or not. It is God's gift to you to keep you sensitive to his moral code. But you must use the gift. If you don't listen to and obey your conscience, it will become harder and harder to hear it. Your conscience can malfunction if not properly cared for. It can condemn you too harshly or let you off too easily. Your conscience will only function effectively if you stay close to God, spend time in his Word, and make an effort to understand yourself and your own tendencies toward right and wrong. If your conscience is working faithfully, it will tell your heart and mind the difference between what is right and wrong. You will have a strong inner sense, a voice of accountability, guiding you to do what is right. If your conscience has become dull or inactive, you will find yourself not always doing the right thing or being unmoved by evil. Praying and reading God's Word will sharpen and sensitize your conscience so that it clearly speaks the truth and keeps you in sync with God.

DIVINE PROMISE

MY CONSCIENCE IS CLEAR, BUT THAT DOESN'T
PROVE I'M RIGHT. IT IS THE LORD HIMSELF
WHO WILL EXAMINE ME AND DECIDE.
1 Corinthians 4:4

Consequences

MY QUESTION *for* GOD

If I ask God to forgive me, do I still have to experience the consequences of my actions?

A MOMENT *with* GOD

Your own actions have brought this upon you. This punishment is bitter, piercing you to the heart!

JEREMIAH 4:18

I am waiting for you, O Lord. You must answer
for me, O Lord my God. . . . I am on the verge of
collapse, facing constant pain. But I confess my sins;
I am deeply sorry for what I have done. . . . Come
quickly to help me, O Lord my savior.

Psalm 38:15-18, 22

Those who live only to satisfy their own sinful nature
will harvest decay and death from that sinful nature.
But those who live to please the Spirit will harvest
everlasting life from the Spirit.   Galatians 6:8

❧

*I*f you fall down the steps and break your arm, you
can't press a rewind button and try walking down
those steps again without falling. Your arm is broken,
and you must go through the healing process. Unfortunately, sometimes we do things a lot worse than breaking an arm. When you do something you later regret,
you almost always will suffer the consequences of your
actions. God doesn't rush in and press the rewind button. He usually lets the consequences of your actions
run their course because he wants you to learn and
grow from your mistakes. If he swooped in to save you
every time you messed up, you'd never learn. You'd
become a spoiled brat, not caring if you hurt others
because you never feel any remorse for what you do.
Even if God does not take away the consequences, he
does heal the hurt. Just like a broken bone heals over
time if you take proper care of it, so God heals the hurt
in your life and in the life of anyone you've wronged.
He does this in many ways, but the most powerful way

is through forgiveness. When you have hurt someone and then ask that person to forgive you, a miraculous healing begins to take place in your relationship. In the same way, when you ask God to forgive your sinful actions, a miraculous healing takes place in your relationship with him. Just as a broken bone will actually heal and be stronger than before, so forgiveness can heal relationships and make them stronger than ever. But it is only through experiencing the consequences of your actions that these positive changes can take place.

DIVINE CHALLENGE

DO WHAT IS RIGHT AND GOOD IN THE LORD'S SIGHT, SO ALL WILL GO WELL WITH YOU.

Deuteronomy 6:18

Contentment

MY QUESTION *for* GOD

How can I be more content?

A MOMENT *with* GOD

Don't love money; be satisfied with what you have. For God has said, "I will never fail you. I will never abandon you."   HEBREWS 13:5

Not that I was ever in need, for I have learned how to be content with whatever I have. I know how to live on almost nothing or with everything. I have learned the secret of living in every situation, whether it is with a full stomach or empty, with plenty or little. For I can do everything through Christ, who gives me strength.   PHILIPPIANS 4:11-13

*M*ost of us tend to equate contentment with having every material thing we think we need and want in life to be happy. No wonder we get rattled when life goes sour and material things don't satisfy. True contentment actually has nothing to do with material goods or perfect circumstances. True contentment only comes from the peace and love God offers, and it remains secure despite life's circumstances. Contentment settles upon your heart when you meditate on God's Word and give him control of your life.

DIVINE PROMISE

YOU WILL KEEP IN PERFECT PEACE ALL WHO TRUST IN YOU, ALL WHOSE THOUGHTS ARE FIXED ON YOU!   *Isaiah 26:3*

Conversation

MY QUESTION *for* GOD

How can I live my life in conversation with God?

A MOMENT *with* GOD

So my God gave me the idea to call together all the nobles and leaders of the city, along with the ordinary citizens, for registration.   NEHEMIAH 7:5

Be careful that you do not refuse to listen to the One who is speaking. For if the people of Israel did not escape when they refused to listen to Moses, the earthly messenger, we will certainly not escape if we reject the One who speaks to us from heaven!

HEBREWS 12:25

Nehemiah gave God credit for the idea of registering the people. This is different from the way some people say, "The Lord told me . . ." to support their actions or opinions. Rather, Nehemiah had a constant sense of God's presence. His life was a moment-by-moment conversation with God, even as he energetically pursued an ambitious agenda. How can you be more aware of God speaking to you? Try sticking a note on your computer reminding you to say a quick prayer whenever you sit down to work. Or set an alarm on your cell phone to sound every sixty minutes; when it goes off, take thirty seconds to review how the Lord has been with you in the last hour, and ask him to help you in the hour ahead. Take time to listen to God too. When you do, your relationship will grow as a result of fulfilling conversation. You will have one divine moment after another as you continually converse with God.

DIVINE PROMISE

DIVINE PROMISE

COME AND LISTEN TO MY COUNSEL. I'LL SHARE
MY HEART WITH YOU AND MAKE YOU WISE.
Proverbs 1:23

Convictions

MY QUESTION *for* GOD

How do convictions strengthen my faith?

A MOMENT *with* GOD

Daniel was determined not to defile himself by eating
the food and wine given to them by the king. He
asked the chief of staff for permission not to eat these
unacceptable foods. DANIEL 1:8

This will continue until we all come to such unity in
our faith and knowledge of God's Son that we will
be mature in the Lord, measuring up to the full and
complete standard of Christ. Then we will no longer
be immature like children. We won't be tossed and
blown about by every wind of new teaching. We will
not be influenced when people try to trick us with
lies so clever they sound like the truth. Instead, we
will speak the truth in love, growing in every way
more and more like Christ, who is the head of his
body, the church. EPHESIANS 4:13-15

Conviction is more than just belief; it is commitment to a belief. What you think, say, and do reveals the strength of your convictions. For example, when you believe that Jesus Christ is who he claims to be, then you should have the conviction to live by his teachings. Convictions prepare you to effectively live out your faith and to defend your faith when necessary. *Conviction* can also refer to the work of the Holy Spirit in your heart, telling you what is right and wrong. Without the Holy Spirit convicting you, you would be unprepared to face temptation and would easily give in when your faith is challenged. Convictions hold you steady on the path of life and help you to faithfully live and act out your faith in practical ways. If you keep your convictions sharp by reading God's Word, your life will be a great story of faith.

DIVINE PROMISE

LET THE HOLY SPIRIT GUIDE YOUR LIVES. THEN YOU WON'T BE DOING WHAT YOUR SINFUL NATURE CRAVES. THE SINFUL NATURE WANTS TO DO EVIL, WHICH IS JUST THE OPPOSITE OF WHAT THE SPIRIT WANTS. AND THE SPIRIT GIVES US DESIRES THAT ARE THE OPPOSITE OF WHAT THE SINFUL NATURE DESIRES.

Galatians 5:16-17

Courage

MY QUESTION *for* GOD

Where can I find the courage to go on when life gets too hard?

A MOMENT *with* GOD

The LORD your God . . . is with you!

DEUTERONOMY 20:1

The LORD is my light and my salvation—so why should I be afraid?   PSALM 27:1

Be strong and courageous! Do not be afraid or discouraged. For the LORD your God is with you wherever you go.   JOSHUA 1:9

Don't be afraid, for I am with you. Don't be discouraged, for I am your God. I will strengthen you and help you. I will hold you up with my victorious right hand.   ISAIAH 41:10

Throughout your lifetime, you will find yourself in scary situations—extreme stress, major illness, financial difficulties, even mortal danger. True courage comes from understanding that God is stronger than your biggest problem or your worst enemy. God wants to help you by giving you his power. Courage does not come from misplaced confidence in your own strength but from well-placed confidence in God's strength. Fear comes from feeling alone against a great threat; courage comes from knowing God is beside you, helping you fight that threat. As you focus on God's

presence, you will build up the courage you need to go
on and face whatever lies ahead.

DIVINE PROMISE

HAVING HOPE WILL GIVE YOU COURAGE. YOU
WILL BE PROTECTED AND WILL REST IN SAFETY.
Job 11:18

Creativity

MY QUESTION *for* GOD

What is creativity?

A MOMENT *with* GOD

Beautiful words stir my heart. I will recite a lovely
poem about the king, for my tongue is like the pen of
a skillful poet.   PSALM 45:1

Why do artists paint, authors write, and musicians
play instruments? Because these are the unique ways
they express themselves. Creativity is the overflow of
a full heart and mind. But sometimes we're empty, or
we're full of the wrong material. How can you be full
of the kind of beauty that spills out in wonderful and
meaningful ideas, sounds, words, and movements? By
taking the time to fill up on what is beautiful and what
is true. If creativity is to express the beauty of God,
then you must always be filling up on God's Spirit and

his wisdom. Take time to know God. Soak up what is beautiful. Think about God and all his creative works in the world around you. As your heart and mind fill up with him, you can be sure that the creativity will flow out of your life in productive ways.

DIVINE PROMISE

FIX YOUR THOUGHTS ON WHAT IS TRUE, AND HONORABLE, AND RIGHT, AND PURE, AND LOVELY, AND ADMIRABLE. THINK ABOUT THINGS THAT ARE EXCELLENT AND WORTHY OF PRAISE. KEEP PUTTING INTO PRACTICE ALL YOU LEARNED AND RECEIVED FROM ME—EVERYTHING YOU HEARD FROM ME AND SAW ME DOING. THEN THE GOD OF PEACE WILL BE WITH YOU. *Philippians 4:8-9*

Crisis

MY QUESTION *for* GOD

Where is God in my time of crisis?

A MOMENT *with* GOD

By means of their suffering, he rescues those who suffer. For he gets their attention through adversity.

JOB 36:15

The LORD hears the cries of the needy; he does not despise his imprisoned people. PSALM 69:33

Can anything ever separate us from Christ's love?
Does it mean he no longer loves us if we have
trouble or calamity, or are persecuted, or hungry,
or destitute, or in danger, or threatened with death?

ROMANS 8:35

I have told you all this so that you may have peace
in me. Here on earth you will have many trials and
sorrows. But take heart, because I have overcome
the world.   JOHN 16:33

*Y*ou don't need to pray that God would be with you
in times of crisis—he is already there. Instead, pray
that you will recognize God's presence and have the
humility and discernment to accept his help. God does
not say he will prevent times of crisis in your life; this
is a fallen world where terrible things happen. But
God does promise to be there with you and for you—
always—helping you through any crisis you face. He
promises to guide you toward peace and hope in the
midst of your crisis. He also promises to bring you to
heaven, where all trouble and crisis will end forever.

DIVINE PROMISE

GOD IS OUR REFUGE AND STRENGTH, ALWAYS
READY TO HELP IN TIMES OF TROUBLE. SO WE
WILL NOT FEAR WHEN EARTHQUAKES COME
AND THE MOUNTAINS CRUMBLE INTO THE SEA.
LET THE OCEANS ROAR AND FOAM. LET THE
MOUNTAINS TREMBLE AS THE WATERS SURGE!

Psalm 46:1-3

Culture

MY QUESTION *for* GOD

How does my culture affect me?

A MOMENT *with* GOD

Don't copy the behavior and customs of this world, but let God transform you into a new person by changing the way you think. Then you will learn to know God's will for you, which is good and pleasing and perfect. ROMANS 12:2

Think about how the weather affects your life every day. The temperature, precipitation, wind, and other factors affect what you choose to wear and the activities you choose to do that day. The weather can even affect your attitude. If it is dark and gloomy, you might feel depressed or tired. If it is a brilliant sunny day, you might feel happy and energetic. Adjusting to the weather is something you hardly notice unless you stop to think about it. Similarly, our culture affects us every day—far more than you may realize. It will impact almost everything you do. Culture plays a subtle but powerful role in influencing your values, beliefs, and actions. The culture you live in takes on a personality of its own, pressuring you to conform and fit in, challenging what you believe, and even shaming you into compliance. As a result, without even realizing it, you may be adopting lifestyle choices that are disappointing to God. To follow God's will, you have to know his will by becoming familiar with his Word. Your life can be transformed by allowing God to challenge your worldview and change the way you think about and respond to your culture.

DIVINE PROMISE

YOU ARE THE LIGHT OF THE WORLD—LIKE A CITY ON A HILLTOP THAT CANNOT BE HIDDEN. NO ONE LIGHTS A LAMP AND THEN PUTS IT UNDER A BASKET. INSTEAD, A LAMP IS PLACED ON A STAND, WHERE IT GIVES LIGHT TO EVERYONE IN THE HOUSE. IN THE SAME WAY, LET YOUR GOOD DEEDS SHINE OUT FOR ALL TO SEE, SO THAT EVERYONE WILL PRAISE YOUR HEAVENLY FATHER. *Matthew 5:14-16*

Danger

MY QUESTION *for* GOD

What is one danger I should be on the lookout for?

A MOMENT *with* GOD

Dear children, keep away from anything that might take God's place in your hearts.   1 JOHN 5:21

Stay alert! Watch out for your great enemy, the devil. He prowls around like a roaring lion, looking for someone to devour.   1 PETER 5:8

*T*emptation to do wrong is one of the greatest dangers you face. When you're driving on a country road, the purpose of a guardrail on a dangerous curve is not to inhibit your freedom but to save your life! That guardrail is an object of security and safety, not an obstacle to driving. In the same way, you need a guardrail as you travel through life—not to inhibit your freedom but to help you avoid danger and keep your life from going out of control. Your heart helps determine where you go because it affects your passions. If you don't guard your heart with God's Word and stay focused on the road God has put you on, you may have a terrible accident when temptation distracts you. Satan is constantly on the attack, trying to tempt you to sin against God. You may give in sometimes—we all do. When you throw caution to the wind, you give in to temptation at every turn, and you are in danger of being completely ineffective for God. But if you take caution, you will be more aware of when you are giving in to sin so that you can recognize it, admit it, and correct it.

DIVINE PROMISE

THE WISE ARE CAUTIOUS AND AVOID DANGER;
FOOLS PLUNGE AHEAD WITH RECKLESS
CONFIDENCE.   *Proverbs 14:16*

Decisions

Does every decision I make really matter that much?

Commit your actions to the LORD, and your plans
will succeed.   PROVERBS 16:3

Oh, that we might know the LORD! Let us press on
to know him. He will respond to us as surely as the
arrival of dawn or the coming of rains in early spring.
                                            HOSEA 6:3

My steps have stayed on your path; I have not wavered
from following you.   PSALM 17:5

*M*aking decisions is like hiking: Each step puts you
a little farther down the path. Wrong decisions lead
you down the wrong path, and right decisions lead you
down the right path. Sometimes the right decision is
simply being faithful in the little things. God's will
for you each day is to obey him, serve others, read his
Word, and do what is right. When you have been faithful over time, you will come to a point where you feel
that God is allowing you to choose between several
good options. Stay close enough to God so that you can
recognize his leading in your life. Then it will be easier
to make the right decisions.

DIVINE PROMISE

SEEK HIS WILL IN ALL YOU DO, AND HE WILL
SHOW YOU WHICH PATH TO TAKE. *Proverbs 3:6*

Demands

MY QUESTION *for* GOD

How can I cope when life's demands seem impossible?

A MOMENT *with* GOD

The waves of death overwhelmed me; floods of
destruction swept over me. The grave wrapped its
ropes around me; death laid a trap in my path. But
in my distress I cried out to the LORD; yes, I cried
to my God for help.   2 SAMUEL 22:5-7

Deeper and deeper I sink into the mire; I can't
find a foothold. I am in deep water, and the floods
overwhelm me.   PSALM 69:2

I am exhausted and completely crushed. My groans
come from an anguished heart.   PSALM 38:8

I cry out to the LORD; I plead for the LORD's mercy.
I pour out my complaints before him and tell him all
my troubles. When I am overwhelmed, you alone
know the way I should turn.   PSALM 142:1-3

Everyone goes through times in their lives when the
demands seem impossible. The task is too hard, the

burden too much to bear, the schedule too full to keep up with. Sometimes only your faith keeps you going because you know your greatest source of help is your almighty God—the God of the impossible. When life's demands pile up, your only option is to turn to God, acknowledge your needs, and give up control of your life to him. When you allow God to carry the burden for you, he will give you the strength to continue.

DIVINE PROMISE

HE GIVES POWER TO THE WEAK AND STRENGTH TO THE POWERLESS. EVEN YOUTHS WILL BECOME WEAK AND TIRED, AND YOUNG MEN WILL FALL IN EXHAUSTION. BUT THOSE WHO TRUST IN THE LORD WILL FIND NEW STRENGTH. THEY WILL SOAR HIGH ON WINGS LIKE EAGLES. THEY WILL RUN AND NOT GROW WEARY. THEY WILL WALK AND NOT FAINT.

Isaiah 40:29-31

Desires

MY QUESTION *for* GOD

How do my desires affect me?

A MOMENT *with* GOD

Clothe yourself with the presence of the Lord Jesus Christ. And don't let yourself think about ways to indulge your evil desires.   ROMANS 13:14

As the deer longs for streams of water, so I long for
you, O God. I thirst for God, the living God. When
can I go and stand before him?   PSALM 42:1-2

Whom have I in heaven but you? I desire you more
than anything on earth.   PSALM 73:25

LORD, we show our trust in you by obeying your
laws; our heart's desire is to glorify your name. All
night long I search for you; in the morning I earnestly
seek for God.   ISAIAH 26:8-9

You are motivated by what you really want. A golfer
may strive for the perfect drive; an artist, for rave re-
views; a business executive, for higher profit margins;
a student, for straight A's. An examination of the things
you really desire reveals the priorities of your heart. Your
chances of accomplishing your goals increase in proportion to the intensity of your commitment. Remarkably,
the Bible tells us it is possible for human beings to know
and experience the God of the universe in a personal way.
What more lofty goal could you aspire to? God desires
an intimate and transforming relationship with you. To
experience him, you must desire him with all your heart.
Ask yourself, "Is God just one of my many pursuits, or is
God chief of all my desires?" Or ask your friends if they
think the desire of your heart is a relationship with God.
What would other people guess is your greatest desire?
When you desire God more than anything, your chances
of accomplishing great things for him through his power
increase as you intensify your commitment to him.

DIVINE PROMISE

GOD IS WORKING IN YOU, GIVING YOU
THE DESIRE AND THE POWER TO DO WHAT
PLEASES HIM.   *Philippians 2:13*

Desires

MY QUESTION *for* GOD

How do I know if my desires are right or wrong?

A MOMENT *with* GOD

One day when Samson was in Timnah, one of the
Philistine women caught his eye. When he returned
home, he told his father and mother, "A young
Philistine woman in Timnah caught my eye. I want
to marry her. Get her for me." His father and mother
objected. "Isn't there even one woman in our tribe
or among all the Israelites you could marry?" they
asked. "Why must you go to the pagan Philistines to
find a wife?" But Samson told his father, "Get her for
me! She looks good to me."   JUDGES 14:1-3

Fix your thoughts on what is true, and honorable,
and right, and pure, and lovely, and admirable. Think
about things that are excellent and worthy of praise.

PHILIPPIANS 4:8

Sinful desires are very powerful because they are
selfish. The desire to get what you want is so strong

that it can keep you from thinking straight. Samson saw a beautiful woman and became consumed with having her. It was as if his brain froze up; he didn't even think about all the problems that would come from the relationship. Like Samson, you can become so obsessed with what you want that you forget to ask God if it is what he wants. Make sure that the object of your desire is consistent with God's Word, good for you, and not harmful to others.

DIVINE PROMISE

IF YOU ARE WISE AND UNDERSTAND GOD'S WAYS, PROVE IT BY LIVING AN HONORABLE LIFE, DOING GOOD WORKS WITH THE HUMILITY THAT COMES FROM WISDOM.   *James 3:13*

Determination

MY QUESTION *for* GOD

How is determination a key tool in obtaining spiritual victory?

A MOMENT *with* GOD

A final word: Be strong in the Lord and in his mighty power. Put on all of God's armor so that you will be able to stand firm against all strategies of the devil. For we are not fighting against flesh-and-blood enemies, but against evil rulers and authorities of the unseen world, against mighty powers in this dark world, and against evil spirits in the heavenly places.

EPHESIANS 6:10-12

We have been rescued from our enemies so we can
serve God without fear.   LUKE 1:74

*D*etermination is often the key to winning the battles
of life. Too often Satan is more determined to keep a
foothold in your life than you are to drive him away.
God's people should not be outmatched in the area of
resolve. Your enemies may sometimes be people, but
you will always have spiritual enemies. Are you as determined to fight off evil as Satan is to tempt you with
it? Here are four keys to increasing your determination: (1) Confidence. Recognize that God is mightier
than Satan and will indeed defeat him. (2) Strategy.
Understand Satan's tactics in order to deter him.
(3) Prayer. Call on God to fill you with the power of
his Spirit. (4) Understanding. Know Scripture, claim
God's promises of victory, and realize the blessings and
benefits of victory. You defeat your enemies by being
more determined and more confident than they are.
Through God's strength, you find the determination
and power to defeat those who fight against you. This
gives you the courage and confidence to persevere because you know that God promises ultimate victory to
all who believe in him and obey him.

DIVINE PROMISE

THE LORD IS FAITHFUL; HE WILL STRENGTHEN
YOU AND GUARD YOU FROM THE EVIL ONE.
2 Thessalonians 3:3

Disapproval

MY QUESTION *for* GOD

How can I befriend others when I disapprove of their immoral lifestyles?

A MOMENT *with* GOD

When Jesus came by, he looked up at Zacchaeus and called him by name. "Zacchaeus!" he said. "Quick, come down! I must be a guest in your home today." Zacchaeus quickly climbed down and took Jesus to his house in great excitement and joy. But the people were displeased. "He has gone to be the guest of a notorious sinner," they grumbled. . . . Jesus responded, " . . . The Son of Man came to seek and save those who are lost."   LUKE 19:5-10

If you have pictured Jesus as enjoying the company of only "good," churchgoing people and being too holy to hang out with immoral people, you are mistaken. Jesus found those who appeared to be the furthest from him and ministered to their needs. Following Jesus' example means looking past people's behavior to their souls. It takes special effort to love those you disapprove of, but they are the people who most need a godly friend. Your faith in God and your obedience to his ways shouldn't separate you from the ungodly—in fact, it qualifies you to reach out to them and serve them in love.

DIVINE PROMISE

EVEN THE SON OF MAN CAME NOT TO BE
SERVED BUT TO SERVE OTHERS AND TO GIVE
HIS LIFE AS A RANSOM FOR MANY.   *Matthew 20:28*

Discouragement

MY QUESTION *for* GOD

How can I overcome my feelings of discouragement?

A MOMENT *with* GOD

Elijah replied, "I have zealously served the LORD God
Almighty. But the people of Israel have broken their
covenant with you, torn down your altars, and killed
every one of your prophets. I am the only one left,
and now they are trying to kill me, too."   1 KINGS 19:10

Discouragement can make you feel sorry for yourself.
Don't allow yourself to think you are the only one who
is going through troubles. It can be comforting to realize
that others are going through the same thing you are.

Hannah was in deep anguish, crying bitterly as she
prayed to the LORD.   1 SAMUEL 1:10

Prayer is the best thing to do when you feel discouraged. It brings you near to God, allowing you to be
honest and share your burdens with him. With God

by your side, you're never alone. He will give you the strength and courage you need to get through.

Don't be discouraged by this mighty army, for the battle is not yours, but God's.   2 CHRONICLES 20:15

*L*ike the people of Judah, who could see only a vast enemy army but not God standing by to destroy it, it's easy to focus on your problems and forget that God is near and ready to help. Don't let your feelings of discouragement shake your assurance of God's love for you. Discouragement can cause you to doubt God's love, drawing you away from your greatest source of help. Realize that God will fight on your behalf and help you succeed as you trust in him.

Watch out for your great enemy, the devil. . . . Stand firm against him, and be strong in your faith. Remember that your Christian brothers and sisters all over the world are going through the same kind of suffering you are.   1 PETER 5:8-9

*W*hen you are discouraged, you are particularly vulnerable to spiritual attack. Take special care to stay close to God by praying and reading the Bible. It is through talking with God and reading his Word that he will provide divine moments of encouragement just when you need them most.

DIVINE PROMISE

BE STRONG AND COURAGEOUS! DO NOT BE
AFRAID OR DISCOURAGED. FOR THE LORD
YOUR GOD IS WITH YOU WHEREVER YOU GO.
Joshua 1:9

Doubt

MY QUESTIONS *for* GOD

*Is it wrong to question what I believe? Can it make me
stronger?*

A MOMENT *with* GOD

John the Baptist, who was in prison, heard about
all the things the Messiah was doing. So he sent his
disciples to ask Jesus, "Are you the Messiah we've
been expecting, or should we keep looking for
someone else?"   MATTHEW 11:2-3

Jesus immediately reached out and grabbed him.
"You have so little faith," Jesus said. "Why did you
doubt me?"   MATTHEW 14:31

David, John the Baptist, Peter, Thomas, and many
other biblical heroes all struggled with doubt. God
doesn't mind when you doubt as long as you are seeking him in the midst of it. Doubt can become sin if it
leads you away from God toward skepticism, cynicism,

or hard-heartedness. But doubt can be beneficial when honest searching leads you closer to God and strengthens your faith. Overcoming doubt and learning the truth are always divine moments when God's presence becomes even more real in your life.

DIVINE PROMISE

WHEN DOUBTS FILLED MY MIND, YOUR
COMFORT GAVE ME RENEWED HOPE
AND CHEER.   *Psalm 94:19*

Emotions

MY QUESTION *for* GOD

How can the power of God help me control my emotions?

A MOMENT *with* GOD

Guard your heart above all else, for it determines the course of your life.   PROVERBS 4:23

I will give you a new heart, and I will put a new spirit in you. I will take out your stony, stubborn heart and give you a tender, responsive heart.   EZEKIEL 36:26

Instead, let the Spirit renew your thoughts and attitudes.   EPHESIANS 4:23

Clothe yourself with the presence of the Lord Jesus
Christ. And don't let yourself think about ways to
indulge your evil desires.   ROMANS 13:14

Emotions are a good gift from God. They are evidence
that you are made in God's image, for the Bible shows
that God himself displays the whole range of emotions,
from anger to zeal. But like any gift from God, emotions can be misused. Instead of a blessing, they can
become a curse. Emotions come from the heart, where
there is a desperate battle going on between your old,
sinful nature and your new, Spirit-controlled nature.
Your heart gets caught in a tug-of-war over your emotions. Your new nature helps you use your emotions
to reflect God's character, which will help you love
and serve people in healthy ways. Your sinful nature,
however, tries to get you to redirect and lose control of
your emotions so you lapse into behavior that is harmful to yourself or other people. When emotions go bad,
they tempt you to impulsively seek the pleasures of sin.
For example, the emotion of love can be a powerful
force for good when it leads you to care for someone in
need. But that same emotion can be a powerful force
for evil if it is allowed to turn into lust or jealous rage.
Learn to understand your emotions and direct them
in ways that are productive, not destructive. The issue isn't the power or intensity of your emotions but
whether they lead you toward God or toward sin.

DIVINE PROMISE

THE HOLY SPIRIT PRODUCES THIS KIND OF FRUIT IN OUR LIVES: LOVE, JOY, PEACE, PATIENCE, KINDNESS, GOODNESS, FAITHFULNESS, GENTLENESS, AND SELF-CONTROL. *Galatians 5:22-23*

Emptiness

MY QUESTION *for* GOD

I have so much, but I still feel empty inside. Where can I find fulfillment?

A MOMENT *with* GOD

Don't be dismayed when the wicked grow rich and their homes become ever more splendid. For when they die, they take nothing with them. Their wealth will not follow them into the grave. PSALM 49:16-17

Riches won't help on the day of judgment, but right living can save you from death. PROVERBS 11:4

Enjoy what you have rather than desiring what you don't have. Just dreaming about nice things is meaningless—like chasing the wind. ECCLESIASTES 6:9

May you experience the love of Christ, though it is too great to understand fully. Then you will be made complete with all the fullness of life and power that comes from God. EPHESIANS 3:19

Why is it that some foods satisfy your hunger for a long time while other foods satisfy you only for a short time before you're hungry again? Material things are like junk food that just doesn't fill you up for long. Things can fill physical space, but they can't fill the space in your soul. Only when your soul is filled will you be truly and deeply satisfied. Feelings of emptiness come when you try to fill yourself with the wrong things; eventually you realize they didn't satisfy for long. This is because real fulfillment comes through a relationship with God. The more you get to know God, the more he fills you with himself and his satisfying blessings, such as love, help, encouragement, peace, and comfort. If you are not filled with God's Spirit and the blessings that come with it, then your heart is like an empty room, waiting to be occupied. When you invite God into your life, you will find true satisfaction and fulfillment.

DIVINE PROMISE

DON'T BE SO CONCERNED ABOUT PERISHABLE THINGS LIKE FOOD. SPEND YOUR ENERGY SEEKING THE ETERNAL LIFE THAT THE SON OF MAN CAN GIVE YOU. FOR GOD THE FATHER HAS GIVEN ME THE SEAL OF HIS APPROVAL. *John 6:27*

Encouragement

MY QUESTION *for* GOD

How does God's gift of encouragement renew my life?

A MOMENT *with* GOD

After the death of Moses the LORD's servant, the LORD spoke to Joshua son of Nun, Moses' assistant. He said, "Moses my servant is dead. Therefore, the time has come for you to lead these people, the Israelites, across the Jordan River into the land I am giving them. I promise you what I promised Moses: 'Wherever you set foot, you will be on land I have given you. . . .' No one will be able to stand against you as long as you live. For I will be with you as I was with Moses. I will not fail you or abandon you."

JOSHUA 1:1-5

*J*oshua's strength and resolve may have weakened as he took over the daunting task of leading the Israelites into a land of giants. So God prepared him—and the rest of the people—with specific words of encouragement. Sometimes you may long for someone to come beside you to encourage and strengthen you. How much better if that someone were God himself! Encouragement gives you the courage to go on, to renew your commitment and resolve. It inspires you with the hope that your task is not in vain, that you can make a difference. God's encouragement is a beautiful gift, a spiritual gift that gives you a renewed desire and commitment to obey him. Like Joshua, you don't find encouragement by looking within or at the circumstances around you but by looking up to your Sovereign God.

BE STRONG AND COURAGEOUS! DO NOT
BE AFRAID OR DISCOURAGED. FOR THE
LORD YOUR GOD IS WITH YOU WHEREVER
YOU GO. *Joshua 1:9*

Endurance

MY QUESTION *for* GOD

How can I keep going when I feel like quitting?

A MOMENT *with* GOD

Everyone will hate you because you are my followers.
But the one who endures to the end will be saved.

MARK 13:13

If we endure hardship, we will reign with him. If we
deny him, he will deny us.   2 TIMOTHY 2:12

I am certain that God, who began the good work
within you, will continue his work until it is finally
finished on the day when Christ Jesus returns.

PHILIPPIANS 1:6

Dear friends, you always followed my instructions
when I was with you. And now that I am away, it is
even more important. Work hard to show the results
of your salvation, obeying God with deep reverence
and fear. For God is working in you, giving you the
desire and the power to do what pleases him.

PHILIPPIANS 2:12-13

*E*ndurance can be compared to running a marathon, a grueling race that covers more than twenty-six miles and seems to take a lifetime to finish! The goals in a marathon are to run the race well, to endure all the challenges along the way, and to finish strong and receive the rewards that come with finishing. Those who finish near the top get tangible rewards such as trophies and cash, but everyone who finishes earns the deep satisfaction of completing one of the toughest races on earth. Life is like a marathon. Endurance is necessary to complete the journey, and there are tangible rewards for finishing strong—an inheritance to pass along, a reputation others can respect, a legacy of faith. But the greatest reward for finishing life well is the prize of spending eternity with God. This reward is given to all those who have faith in Jesus Christ and who endure the challenges of this life—persecution, ridicule, and temptation. Just as marathoners must train hard and build up their endurance to run the race and finish well, so Christians must train and build up endurance to live a life of faith in Jesus and stay strong to the end. When you've built up endurance, you will not collapse during the race but will be able to push on toward the goal of becoming more and more like Jesus. Then you will cross the finish line into heaven and receive all the eternal rewards God has promised.

DIVINE PROMISE

LET'S NOT GET TIRED OF DOING WHAT IS GOOD. AT JUST THE RIGHT TIME WE WILL REAP A HARVEST OF BLESSING IF WE DON'T GIVE UP.

Galatians 6:9

Enemies

MY QUESTION *for* GOD

What does it mean to love my enemies?

A MOMENT *with* GOD

You have heard the law that says, "Love your
neighbor" and hate your enemy. But I say, love your
enemies! Pray for those who persecute you!

MATTHEW 5:43-44

All of you should be of one mind. Sympathize with
each other. Love each other as brothers and sisters.
Be tenderhearted, and keep a humble attitude. Don't
repay evil for evil. Don't retaliate with insults when
people insult you. Instead, pay them back with a
blessing. That is what God has called you to do, and
he will bless you for it.   1 PETER 3:8-9

Showing love to your enemies seems completely un-
reasonable—unless you realize that you were once an
enemy of God until he forgave you. When you love your
enemy, you see that person as Jesus does—someone in
need of grace and forgiveness. Getting to that point
requires prayer. When you pray for others, you can't
help but feel compassion for them. Through prayer and
God's grace, you might turn an enemy into a friend.

DIVINE CHALLENGE

IF YOUR ENEMIES ARE HUNGRY, FEED THEM. IF
THEY ARE THIRSTY, GIVE THEM SOMETHING
TO DRINK. . . . DON'T LET EVIL CONQUER YOU,
BUT CONQUER EVIL BY DOING GOOD.
Romans 12:20-21

Energy

MY QUESTION *for* GOD

How can I have more energy?

A MOMENT *with* GOD

Work with enthusiasm, as though you were working
for the Lord rather than for people.   EPHESIANS 6:7

When you do your work as though you are doing it
for God, you will have more enthusiasm and energy
because your tasks are infused with divine purpose.

No, dear brothers and sisters, I have not achieved
it, but I focus on this one thing: Forgetting the past
and looking forward to what lies ahead, I press on
to reach the end of the race and receive the heavenly
prize for which God, through Christ Jesus, is
calling us.   PHILIPPIANS 3:13-14

You will have more energy for today and tomorrow
if you don't waste it focusing on the past. The more

baggage you drag around from your past, the heavier the load you carry today and the less energy you have. God's Word tells you to let it go. Free yourself from the past, and funnel your energy into making today and tomorrow everything God has planned for you.

No discipline is enjoyable while it is happening— it's painful! But afterward there will be a peaceful harvest of right living for those who are trained in this way. So take a new grip with your tired hands and strengthen your weak knees.   HEBREWS 12:11-12

*W*hen you know you are doing the right thing, it can rejuvenate you because you are assured that God is pleased with your actions.

DIVINE PROMISE

MY HEALTH MAY FAIL, AND MY SPIRIT MAY
GROW WEAK, BUT GOD REMAINS THE
STRENGTH OF MY HEART; HE IS MINE FOREVER.
Psalm 73:26

Eternity

MY QUESTION *for* GOD

How should my hope of eternal life affect the way I live now?

A MOMENT *with* GOD

What do you benefit if you gain the whole world but lose your own soul? Is anything worth more than your soul?
MARK 8:36-37

Then [Jesus] said, "Beware! Guard against every kind of greed. Life is not measured by how much you own." Then he told them a story: "A rich man had a fertile farm that produced fine crops. He said to himself, 'What should I do? I don't have room for all my crops.' Then he said, 'I know! I'll tear down my barns and build bigger ones. Then I'll have room enough to store all my wheat and other goods. And I'll sit back and say to myself, "My friend, you have enough stored away for years to come. Now take it easy! Eat, drink, and be merry!"' But God said to him, 'You fool! You will die this very night. Then who will get everything you worked for?' Yes, a person is a fool to store up earthly wealth but not have a rich relationship with God."
LUKE 12:15-21

*I*f the rewards of this earthly life were the only thing we had to live for, a "why bother" attitude might be understandable. But this perspective is mistaken. When you try to obey God, you put yourself in a position to enjoy life the way it is meant to be enjoyed. Your relationships are more fulfilling because people can trust you. Your life is happier because you are avoiding many of the consequences of sin. You feel more secure because you know where you are going after you die.

[Jesus] said, "If any of you wants to be my follower, you must turn from your selfish ways, take up your cross, and follow me. If you try to hang on to your life, you will lose it. But if you give up your life for my sake and for the sake of the Good News, you will save it."   MARK 8:34-35

Those who belong to Christ Jesus have nailed the passions and desires of their sinful nature to his cross and crucified them there.   GALATIANS 5:24

When you believe that Jesus died on the cross to spare you from eternal punishment and give you the free gift of eternal life, then the troubles of this life are put in perspective. You know that your eternal future is secure. This gives you peace no matter what happens in this life, and it changes the way you react to the troubles and trials life throws your way. Your sinful nature no longer controls you; you are free to live as God wants you to live.

DIVINE PROMISE

GOD LOVED THE WORLD SO MUCH THAT
HE GAVE HIS ONE AND ONLY SON, SO THAT
EVERYONE WHO BELIEVES IN HIM WILL NOT
PERISH BUT HAVE ETERNAL LIFE. *John 3:16*

Evil

MY QUESTION *for* GOD

If God is good, why does he allow evil in the world?

A MOMENT *with* GOD

The LORD God placed the man in the Garden of Eden to tend and watch over it. But the LORD God warned him, "You may freely eat the fruit of every tree in the garden—except the tree of the knowledge of good and evil. If you eat its fruit, you are sure to die."

GENESIS 2:15-17

Stay alert! Watch out for your great enemy, the devil. He prowls around like a roaring lion, looking for someone to devour. Stand firm against him, and be strong in your faith.   1 PETER 5:8-9

Then I went into your sanctuary, O God, and I finally understood the destiny of the wicked. Truly, you put them on a slippery path and send them sliding over the cliff to destruction. In an instant they are destroyed, completely swept away by terrors. When you arise, O Lord, you will laugh at their silly ideas as a person laughs at dreams in the morning.

PSALM 73:17-20

Genuine love requires the freedom to choose. From the beginning, God gave us this freedom because he loves us so much and desires a relationship with us. But with the ability to make choices comes the possibility of choosing your own way instead of God's way. When we choose our own way, it always leads to sin because we are all born with a sinful nature. This breaks God's heart. But if he hadn't given us the freedom to choose, he would have created robots, not humans. Evil still exists, and evil people continue to do evil things because they choose to. But you can choose to do what is right. When you do, God is greatly pleased, good prevails, and Satan loses ground. Eventually God will completely destroy the power of evil forever. Until that day, you can overcome evil by choosing to obey God.

DIVINE CHALLENGE

DON'T LET ANYONE CAPTURE YOU WITH EMPTY PHILOSOPHIES AND HIGH-SOUNDING NONSENSE THAT COME FROM HUMAN THINKING AND FROM THE SPIRITUAL POWERS OF THIS WORLD, RATHER THAN FROM CHRIST.

Colossians 2:8

Example

MY QUESTION *for* GOD

What kind of qualities will make others look up to me?

A MOMENT *with* GOD

Whoever wants to be a leader among you must be your servant.   MATTHEW 20:26

EXAMPLE   103

I pressed further, "What you are doing is not right!"

NEHEMIAH 5:9 .

He must become greater and greater, and I must
become less and less.   JOHN 3:30

*I*f you want to be looked up to by your peers, be a
godly example for them. Have a servant's heart, take
responsibility for your actions, don't pass the buck
when it's convenient, refuse to stay silent when something is wrong, and stay humble. The world teaches
you to look and act cool, to use foul language, to dis-
respect authority, and to bend the rules as far as you
can. But the Bible teaches the opposite. In the end it
will be the people who have consistently lived lives of
kindness, integrity, and a deep love for God who will
be the most respected and honored.

DIVINE CHALLENGE

YOU ARE THE LIGHT OF THE WORLD—LIKE A
CITY ON A HILLTOP THAT CANNOT BE HIDDEN.
. . . IN THE SAME WAY, LET YOUR GOOD DEEDS
SHINE OUT FOR ALL TO SEE, SO THAT EVERYONE
WILL PRAISE YOUR HEAVENLY FATHER.

Matthew 5:14, 16

Excellence

MY QUESTION *for* GOD

Why is it important to strive for excellence?

A MOMENT *with* GOD

Then God looked over all he had made, and he saw
that it was very good!   GENESIS 1:31

Do you have the gift of helping others? Do it with all
the strength and energy that God supplies.   1 PETER 4:11

Hezekiah encouraged all the Levites regarding the
skill they displayed as they served the LORD.
                                          2 CHRONICLES 30:22

The LORD has filled Bezalel with the Spirit of God,
giving him great wisdom, ability, and expertise in all
kinds of crafts. He is a master craftsman, expert in
working with gold, silver, and bronze. . . . And the
LORD has given both him and Oholiab . . . the ability
to teach their skills to others.   EXODUS 35:31-34

God set the standard for excellence. No machine can
ever duplicate the marvelous complexity that God created in the human body. No artist can paint a picture
that rivals one of God's real-life sunsets. God wants us
to pursue excellence because doing so shows that we
care about doing things right and about helping others
to the best of our ability. Pursuing excellence helps
others experience excellence, giving them a glimpse
of God's character and inspiring them to pursue ex-

cellence themselves. God initiated excellence in the beauty of his creation, and we are called to perpetuate it. We do this first by striving to accomplish God's will in our lives. Our lives display excellence when we consistently strive to model ourselves after Jesus Christ, who was perfect, and when we go about the work he has called us to do. We'll never be perfect in this life, but as we work toward that goal, we will model excellence to those around us.

DIVINE PROMISE

WORK WILLINGLY AT WHATEVER YOU DO, AS THOUGH YOU WERE WORKING FOR THE LORD RATHER THAN FOR PEOPLE. REMEMBER THAT THE LORD WILL GIVE YOU AN INHERITANCE AS YOUR REWARD, AND THAT THE MASTER YOU ARE SERVING IS CHRIST. *Colossians 3:23-24*

Experience

MY QUESTION *for* GOD

How do I develop the experience I need to be an effective witness for God?

A MOMENT *with* GOD

He took David from tending the ewes and lambs and made him the shepherd of Jacob's descendants— God's own people, Israel. He cared for them with a true heart and led them with skillful hands.

PSALM 78:71-72

$\mathcal{D}$o the best you can wherever you are. Remember that God wastes nothing but uses everything to further his good purposes. David's first job was shepherding—hardly the recommended grooming for a future king! Yet the lessons David learned on the hills with the sheep served him well on the throne; he ruled not as a tyrant but as a shepherd. God will use you in whatever situation your find yourself, and he will use your current circumstances to prepare you for future service. If you feel like your classes, extracurriculars, or job aren't significant now, remember that God is preparing you for service later. Make the most of where God has put you right now. God wants to use you both now and later. Serving God right where you are can be a divine moment of preparation for where God wants to eventually move you.

DIVINE PROMISE

I AM CERTAIN THAT GOD, WHO BEGAN THE GOOD WORK WITHIN YOU, WILL CONTINUE HIS WORK UNTIL IT IS FINALLY FINISHED ON THE DAY WHEN CHRIST JESUS RETURNS.

Philippians 1:6

$\mathcal{F}ailure$

MY QUESTION *for* GOD

What is failure in God's eyes?

A MOMENT *with* GOD

What do you benefit if you gain the whole world but lose your own soul? Is anything worth more than your soul?
MATTHEW 16:26

Anyone who listens to my teaching and follows it is wise, like a person who builds a house on solid rock. Though the rain comes in torrents and the floodwaters rise and the winds beat against that house, it won't collapse because it is built on bedrock. But anyone who hears my teaching and doesn't obey it is foolish, like a person who builds a house on sand. When the rains and floods come and the winds beat against that house, it will collapse with a mighty crash.
MATTHEW 7:24-27

It's your sins that have cut you off from God. Because of your sins, he has turned away and will not listen anymore.
ISAIAH 59:2

If you make straight A's, receive the most valuable player award, get elected class president, or hang out with the in crowd, would you say your life is a success? God says you would be failing if you do these things apart from him. Failure in God's eyes happens when you fail to live the way he created you to live. God wants you to live a certain way for a very good reason—to help you make the most of life, both now and forever. Sin causes failure because it is contrary to God's plan, and God's plan is always best for you. God gave you the gift of life and created you to have a relationship with him. Your greatest failure would be to reject the God who gave you life or the way of life he wants for you. Don't fail by neglecting or ignoring God.

DIVINE PROMISE

THE LORD DIRECTS THE STEPS OF THE GODLY. HE DELIGHTS IN EVERY DETAIL OF THEIR LIVES. THOUGH THEY STUMBLE, THEY WILL NEVER FALL, FOR THE LORD HOLDS THEM BY THE HAND.   *Psalm 37:23-24*

Faith

MY QUESTION *for* GOD

How should my faith in God affect the way I live?

A MOMENT *with* GOD

I tell you the truth, those who listen to my message and believe in God who sent me have eternal life.

JOHN 5:24

Faith is the confidence that what we hope for will actually happen; it gives us assurance about things we cannot see.   HEBREWS 11:1

Faith is more than just believing; it is entrusting your very life to what you believe. For example, you may *believe* that someone can cross a deep gorge on a tightrope. But would you *trust* that person to carry you across? If you truly had faith, you would say yes. Faith in God means that you are willing to trust him with your whole life. You are willing to follow his guidelines for living, as outlined in the Bible, because you have the conviction that his will is best for you. You are even willing to endure ridicule and persecution for your faith because you are sure that God is who he says he is and he will keep his promises about salvation and eternal life in heaven.

DIVINE PROMISE

BELIEVE IN THE LORD JESUS AND YOU WILL BE SAVED. *Acts 16:31*

Fear

MY QUESTION *for* GOD

What does fear do to me?

A MOMENT *with* GOD

This was their report to Moses: "We entered the land you sent us to explore, and it is indeed a bountiful country—a land flowing with milk and honey. Here is the kind of fruit it produces. But the people living there are powerful, and their towns are large and fortified. We even saw giants there. . . ." But Caleb tried to quiet the people as they stood before Moses. "Let's go at once to take the land," he said. "We can certainly conquer it!" But the other men who had

explored the land with him disagreed. "We can't go
up against them! They are stronger than we are!"

NUMBERS 13:27-31

$\mathcal{F}$ear is real and fear is normal, but fear can paralyze.
When the spies returned from scouting the Promised
Land, the issue they faced was fact versus fear. The
fact was that God had promised that the people would
conquer the land. God himself sent the scouts into the
land, which should have given the people great confidence. Their fear was because of the giants that seemed
more frightening and immediate than God's promise.
Fear distorts your view of reality. The giants in your
path appear more powerful than God, who promises to
deliver you. Sooner or later you'll face fearsome giants
in your life—an especially big temptation, or guilt,
sin, anger, anxiety, depression, etc. When that happens, don't let the size of the giant reduce the size of
your God!

DIVINE PROMISE

I HOLD YOU BY YOUR RIGHT HAND—I, THE
LORD YOUR GOD. AND I SAY TO YOU, "DON'T BE
AFRAID. I AM HERE TO HELP YOU." *Isaiah 41:13*

Feelings

MY QUESTION *for* GOD

How can I learn to control the way I respond to my feelings?

A MOMENT *with* GOD

So I say, let the Holy Spirit guide your lives. Then you won't be doing what your sinful nature craves. The sinful nature wants to do evil, which is just the opposite of what the Spirit wants. And the Spirit gives us desires that are the opposite of what the sinful nature desires. These two forces are constantly fighting each other, so you are not free to carry out your good intentions. But when you are directed by the Holy Spirit, you are no longer subject to the law.

GALATIANS 5:16-18

You're probably aware that your feelings are not a reliable guide because they are so easily influenced. In addition to the normal highs and lows of daily life, your feelings are influenced by something deeper—your sinful nature. But your feelings also have the capacity to be controlled by God's Holy Spirit, who lives inside of you. The best way to know whether you're responding appropriately to your feelings is to let the Holy Spirit control you and to check your reactions against God's Word. These two will never contradict. When you do this, you'll have a clear conscience and greater confidence to deal with whatever feelings your life's circumstances may produce.

DIVINE PROMISE

I PRAY THAT GOD, THE SOURCE OF HOPE, WILL
FILL YOU COMPLETELY WITH JOY AND PEACE
BECAUSE YOU TRUST IN HIM. THEN YOU WILL
OVERFLOW WITH CONFIDENT HOPE THROUGH
THE POWER OF THE HOLY SPIRIT.   *Romans 15:13*

Finishing

MY QUESTION *for* GOD

How can I learn to follow through on my good intentions?

A MOMENT *with* GOD

The LORD was with the people of Judah, and they
took possession of the hill country. But they failed to
drive out the people living in the plains, who had iron
chariots. The town of Hebron was given to Caleb as
Moses had promised. And Caleb drove out the people
living there, who were descendants of the three sons
of Anak.   JUDGES 1:19-20

Finishing is better than starting. Patience is better
than pride.   ECCLESIASTES 7:8

Jesus explained: "My nourishment comes from
doing the will of God, who sent me, and from
finishing his work."   JOHN 4:34

I brought glory to you here on earth by completing
the work you gave me to do.   JOHN 17:4

Don't you realize that in a race everyone runs, but
only one person gets the prize? So run to win!

1 CORINTHIANS 9:24

Few things are as disappointing as good intentions
unrealized. The Israelites, inspired by Joshua's strong
example and godly life, had great intentions to finish
what they had started—conquering the Promised Land.
Unfortunately, the rest of the book of Judges is a sad
story about good intentions that fizzled. There are no
rewards for good intentions. If you intend to follow God
someday but never get around to it, you'll forfeit the
reward of heaven. If you intend to do your homework
every day but never get around to it, you'll never get
the reward of good grades. The greater the intention
for good, the greater the reward when finished. The
key to finishing something—to following through on
your good intentions—is to have a clear picture of the
end goal. When you see clearly where you are going and
what your good intentions can accomplish, you will be
more motivated to follow through. For example, if you
know that writing an encouraging note to a friend will
make that person's day, picture that scene in your mind
until you write the note and send it. When you know
that a kind act will bring glory to God and rewards
to you, picture doing it in your mind until you follow
through. There are amazing rewards in store for those
who follow through with godly intentions. What good
intentions do you have right now to live for God or to
make important changes in your life? Good intentions
take follow-through and perseverance to become reality.

Divine moments often come when you finish the tasks
God puts before you.

DIVINE CHALLENGE

LET US RUN WITH ENDURANCE THE RACE GOD
HAS SET BEFORE US. WE DO THIS BY KEEPING
OUR EYES ON JESUS, THE CHAMPION WHO
INITIATES AND PERFECTS OUR FAITH.

Hebrews 12:1-2

Flexibility

MY QUESTION *for* GOD

*How does being flexible make me available for divine
moments with God?*

A MOMENT *with* GOD

We've given up everything to follow you.

MATTHEW 19:27

If any of you wants to be my follower, you must turn
from your selfish ways, take up your cross, and follow
me. If you try to hang on to your life, you will lose
it. But if you give up your life for my sake and for the
sake of the Good News, you will save it.   MARK 8:34-35

*B*eing flexible allows you to avoid anything that might take your focus off God and to devote yourself to him with all your heart when he calls. This kind of availability for God's use prepares your heart for surprise moments with him as he guides you through life. God blesses you not just because of your ability but because of your availability.

As soon as they landed, they left everything and followed Jesus.

LUKE 5:11

*B*eing flexible shows that you understand the importance of God's timing. It allows room in your life to change your plans. Flexibility means that no matter what you do, you do it with a desire to serve God. Flexibility develops through an eagerness to go where God calls you and serve where he places you.

DIVINE PROMISE

YOU MUST REMAIN FAITHFUL TO WHAT YOU HAVE BEEN TAUGHT FROM THE BEGINNING. IF YOU DO, YOU WILL REMAIN IN FELLOWSHIP WITH THE SON AND WITH THE FATHER. AND IN THIS FELLOWSHIP WE ENJOY THE ETERNAL LIFE HE PROMISED US. *1 John 2:24-25*

Forgiveness

MY QUESTION *for* GOD

How can I experience God's forgiveness?

A MOMENT *with* GOD

Likewise, all the leaders of the priests and the people
became more and more unfaithful. They followed
all the pagan practices of the surrounding nations,
desecrating the Temple of the LORD that had been
consecrated in Jerusalem. The LORD, the God of
their ancestors, repeatedly sent his prophets to warn
them, for he had compassion on his people and his
Temple. But the people mocked these messengers
of God and despised their words. They scoffed at
the prophets until the LORD's anger could no longer
be restrained and nothing could be done. So the
LORD brought the king of Babylon against them. The
Babylonians killed Judah's young men, even chasing
after them into the Temple. They had no pity on the
people, killing both young men and young women,
the old and the infirm. God handed all of them over
to Nebuchadnezzar.   2 CHRONICLES 36:14-17

If my people who are called by my name will humble
themselves and pray and seek my face and turn from
their wicked ways, I will hear from heaven and will
forgive their sins and restore their land.

2 CHRONICLES 7:14

On October 2 the wall was finished—just fifty-two
days after we had begun. When our enemies and

the surrounding nations heard about it, they were frightened and humiliated. They realized this work had been done with the help of our God.

NEHEMIAH 6:15-16

*T*he people of Israel had messed up—big-time. They had so totally turned away from God that even when an enemy army surrounded their city, they didn't think to ask God for help. So God allowed their enemies to defeat them, to destroy the great city of Jerusalem, and to carry off the survivors as slaves into captivity in a foreign land. But that's not the end of the story. God gives second chances. Not only did he forgive his people when they finally realized their sin, but he also put a plan into action to bless them again as he had in the past. He called Nehemiah to be the leader to carry out his plan and provide the encouragement to help the people return to their homeland and rebuild the wall of their city. When you mess up, expect to face the consequences—but then ask God to help you start over again. When your heart is sincere and you truly want forgiveness for your sins, God will give you another chance—again and again. Why? Because more than anything, the almighty God of the universe wants a personal relationship with you. His patient and repeated forgiveness is proof of that.

DIVINE PROMISE

I—YES, I ALONE—WILL BLOT OUT YOUR SINS
FOR MY OWN SAKE AND WILL NEVER THINK
OF THEM AGAIN.   *Isaiah 43:25*

Freedom

MY QUESTION *for* GOD

What is true freedom?

A MOMENT *with* GOD

Against its will, all creation was subjected to God's
curse. But with eager hope, the creation looks forward
to the day when it will join God's children in glorious
freedom from death and decay.   ROMANS 8:20-21

Look, today I am giving you the choice between
a blessing and a curse! You will be blessed if you
obey the commands of the LORD your God that I
am giving you today. But you will be cursed if you
reject the commands of the LORD your God and
turn away from him and worship gods you have not
known before.   DEUTERONOMY 11:26-28

God created human beings with the freedom to choose
to love and obey him and do what is right—or to dis-
obey him and do what is wrong. God gave us this gift
of freedom because without the freedom to choose,
there can be no love. God could have created us so

that we could do only good, eliminating the possibility of evil. But then we would be robots, not humans. It would be coercion, not love. Sin—and therefore evil and death—entered the world through human choice. The Bible tells us how God provides a way for us to be delivered from sin and death. As you read the Bible, let God's Word settle in your heart and mind so that each choice you make today and for the rest of your life will bring you freedom. When you choose to love God in perfect freedom, it is a divine moment in which you see how revolutionary a relationship with him is.

DIVINE PROMISE

SIN IS NO LONGER YOUR MASTER, FOR YOU NO LONGER LIVE UNDER THE REQUIREMENTS OF THE LAW. INSTEAD, YOU LIVE UNDER THE FREEDOM OF GOD'S GRACE.   *Romans 6:14*

Friendship

MY QUESTION *for* GOD

My friendships are really important to me. How can I build friendships that will last?

A MOMENT *with* GOD

David . . . met Jonathan, the king's son. There was an immediate bond between them, for Jonathan loved David. From that day on Saul kept David with him and wouldn't let him return home. And Jonathan

made a solemn pact with David, because he loved
him as he loved himself. Jonathan sealed the pact by
taking off his robe and giving it to David, together
with his tunic, sword, bow, and belt.   1 Samuel 18:1-4

When David and Jonathan met, they immediately became close friends. Their friendship is one of the deepest and closest recorded in the Bible. But they made
an odd pair when you consider that Jonathan was the
king's son and in line for the throne, while David had
been anointed by God to take the throne instead of Jonathan. Jonathan knew this, but he and David were still
best friends. They based their friendship on a common
commitment to honor God. They didn't let anything
come between them. They drew closer together when
their friendship was tested, and they remained friends
to the end. These are the marks of a true friend.

Divine Promise
A FRIEND IS ALWAYS LOYAL.   *Proverbs 17:17*

Fun

My Question *for* God
Can I follow God and still have fun?

A Moment *with* God

For everything there is a season, a time for every
activity under heaven. . . . A time to cry and a time
to laugh. A time to grieve and a time to dance.

ECCLESIASTES 3:1, 4

Go and celebrate with a feast . . . and share gifts of
food with people who have nothing prepared. This is
a sacred day. . . . Don't be dejected and sad, for the
joy of the LORD is your strength!　　　NEHEMIAH 8:10

You have been faithful in handling this small amount.
. . . Let's celebrate together!　　　MATTHEW 25:21

The life of the godly is full of light and joy, but the
light of the wicked will be snuffed out.　　PROVERBS 13:9

*J*udging from the number of feasts and festivals God
instituted for the Israelites, he intended for his people
to have fun. Following God doesn't exclude fun. In
fact, following God's commandments is the way to get
the most out of life—you'll be enjoying life as it was
originally created to be enjoyed. God wants you to have
fun, to enjoy others, and to find joy in your relationship with him. Joy, fun, and celebration are important
aspects of believing in God. These enjoyable experiences lift your spirits and help you see the beauty and
meaning in life. They give you a small taste of the joy
you will experience in heaven. Following God's ways
keeps you from experiencing the sad and painful consequences of sin and allows you to enjoy all the gifts and
benefits of life as it was meant to be lived.

THE GODLY CAN LOOK FORWARD TO A
REWARD, WHILE THE WICKED CAN EXPECT
ONLY JUDGMENT.   *Proverbs 11:23*

Future

MY QUESTION *for* GOD

How can I be more certain about the future?

A MOMENT *with* GOD

The LORD will work out his plans for my life.

PSALM 138:8

I knew you before I formed you in your mother's
womb. Before you were born I set you apart and
appointed you.   JEREMIAH 1:5

We know that God causes everything to work
together for the good of those who love God and are
called according to his purpose for them.   ROMANS 8:28

"I know the plans I have for you," says the LORD.
"They are plans for good and not for disaster, to give
you a future and a hope."   JEREMIAH 29:11

God's plan for your life is not a written script that
you must follow word for word; it's more like a journey with important destinations and appointments but
with a great deal of freedom as to the pace and direc-

tion of travel. The future will always have a sense of mystery about it, but you can be certain that as you look for God's leading, he will guide and direct you on your journey. Your future only becomes uncertain when you separate yourself from God, because then you are removing yourself from his plan, his guidance, and his blessings. But when you come back to him, he will redeem your lost time. Despite all the unknowns and uncertainties ahead, the more you know God, the more certain you will become about your future.

DIVINE PROMISE

TRUST IN THE LORD WITH ALL YOUR HEART; DO NOT DEPEND ON YOUR OWN UNDERSTANDING. SEEK HIS WILL IN ALL YOU DO, AND HE WILL SHOW YOU WHICH PATH TO TAKE. *Proverbs 3:5-6*

Goals

MY QUESTION *for* GOD

What is one of the most important goals I should set for myself?

A MOMENT *with* GOD

Create in me a clean heart, O God. Renew a loyal spirit within me.   PSALM 51:10

Do not despise these small beginnings, for the LORD rejoices to see the work begin.   ZECHARIAH 4:10

Let the Spirit renew your thoughts and attitudes. Put on your new nature, created to be like God.

EPHESIANS 4:23-24

*Y*ou harvest what you plant. Pumpkin seeds produce pumpkins; sunflower seeds produce sunflowers. That is why you must ask the Lord to plant within you a good heart so that your life will produce good thoughts, motives, and actions. If any bad desires or thoughts remain, it is evidence that some bad seeds were planted and you need to do some weeding. Complete renewal is not yet accomplished. None of us will be entirely pure in this life, but purity of mind and heart is one of the most worthy goals to pursue. Set this as one of your goals. Your desire for a clean heart and mind will impact your relationship with God, your family, and your friends more than anything else. How might you be different a year from now—inside and outside— if you make that your goal?

DIVINE PROMISE

LET'S NOT GET TIRED OF DOING WHAT IS GOOD. AT JUST THE RIGHT TIME WE WILL REAP A HARVEST OF BLESSING IF WE DON'T GIVE UP.
Galatians 6:9

Gossip

MY QUESTION *for* GOD

How can I reverse the damage done by gossip?

A MOMENT *with* GOD

A troublemaker plants seeds of strife; gossip separates
the best of friends.   PROVERBS 16:28

Rumors are dainty morsels that sink deep into
one's heart.   PROVERBS 18:8

A gossip goes around telling secrets, so don't hang
around with chatterers.   PROVERBS 20:19

Fire goes out without wood, and quarrels disappear
when gossip stops.   PROVERBS 26:20

It's fun to gossip—it makes us feel like we're letting
others in on our little secrets. The Bible calls gossip
"dainty morsels." The problem is that gossip is based on
rumors, not facts, and the intent of gossip is usually to
damage someone's reputation instead of building it up.
Everyone loves to be in on the latest news, but the very
people with whom you gossip may also be gossiping
about you. Gossip separates friends, reveals people's
secrets, and causes much hurt. Gossip puts you in a
position to judge others. In a court of law, rumors and
opinions are not allowed because they might unjustly
sway the opinion of the jury. So it is when you turn your
classroom or dorm room into a courtroom where you
sit as judge and allow rumors and opinions to damage

the reputations of others who have no chance to defend themselves. You can stop gossip by changing the subject or by saying something kind about the person being targeted. When you don't add fuel to the fire, the fire will go out. Your words might allow God's grace to break through to those around you and may even reach the ears of the person you defend.

DIVINE CHALLENGE

THE SCRIPTURES SAY, "IF YOU WANT TO ENJOY LIFE AND SEE MANY HAPPY DAYS, KEEP YOUR TONGUE FROM SPEAKING EVIL AND YOUR LIPS FROM TELLING LIES." *1 Peter 3:10*

Grace

MY QUESTIONS *for* GOD

Why is God's grace a gift? How do I receive it?

A MOMENT *with* GOD

God saved you by his grace when you believed. And you can't take credit for this; it is a gift from God. Salvation is not a reward for the good things we have done, so none of us can boast about it.   EPHESIANS 2:8-9

The wages of sin is death, but the free gift of God is eternal life through Christ Jesus our Lord.   ROMANS 6:23

We make this plea, not because we deserve help, but because of your mercy.   DANIEL 9:18

$\mathcal{G}$race is like doing a big favor for someone without expecting anything in return. When the Bible says you are saved by grace, it means that God has done you the biggest favor of all—he has pardoned you from the death sentence you deserve because of your sins. You do not have to earn God's grace or work your way into heaven. By grace you are forgiven for your sins and restored to full fellowship with God. Recognizing and requesting God's grace takes humility. The more you realize how much you need God's grace, the more you realize you don't deserve it—which is exactly why you need it! Like the gift of life itself, you cannot take credit for God's grace any more than a baby can brag about being born. The fact that this is God's gift and not the product of your own effort should give you great comfort, security, and hope. Accept God's grace like the gift that it is so you can enjoy its benefits.

DIVINE PROMISE

LET US COME BOLDLY TO THE THRONE OF OUR GRACIOUS GOD. THERE WE WILL RECEIVE HIS MERCY, AND WE WILL FIND GRACE TO HELP US WHEN WE NEED IT MOST.   *Hebrews 4:16*

Guarding Your Heart

MY QUESTIONS *for* GOD

What does it mean to guard my heart? Why is it important?

A MOMENT *with* GOD

Guard your heart above all else, for it determines the
course of your life.   PROVERBS 4:23

I say, anyone who even looks at a woman with lust has
already committed adultery with her in his heart.

MATTHEW 5:28

It is what comes from inside that defiles you. For
from within, out of a person's heart, come evil
thoughts, sexual immorality, . . . lustful desires.

MARK 7:20-22

Your eye is a lamp that provides light for your body.
When your eye is good, your whole body is filled
with light.   LUKE 11:34

The human heart is the most deceitful of all things,
and desperately wicked. Who really knows how bad
it is?   JEREMIAH 17:9

*Y*our actions reveal the condition of your heart because that's where actions begin. Wrong thoughts eventually result in wrong actions if they are left unchecked.
For example, if you think about having sex with someone who is not your spouse, your heart will begin to
convince you that it's okay. Don't trust your emotions
to tell you what is right or good. Trust God's Word—it
comes from God's heart, which is good and perfect.

DIVINE PROMISE

PRAY ABOUT EVERYTHING. TELL GOD WHAT
YOU NEED, AND THANK HIM FOR ALL HE HAS
DONE. THEN YOU WILL EXPERIENCE GOD'S
PEACE, WHICH EXCEEDS ANYTHING WE
CAN UNDERSTAND. HIS PEACE WILL GUARD
YOUR HEARTS AND MINDS AS YOU LIVE IN
CHRIST JESUS.   *Philippians 4:6-7*

Guidance

MY QUESTION *for* GOD

Why doesn't God reveal every part of his plan for my life?

A MOMENT *with* GOD

Your word is a lamp to guide my feet and a light for
my path.   PSALM 119:105

The LORD says, "I will guide you along the best
pathway for your life. I will advise you and watch
over you."   PSALM 32:8

Trust in the LORD with all your heart; do not depend
on your own understanding.   PROVERBS 3:5

The LORD directs the steps of the godly. He delights
in every detail of their lives.   PSALM 37:23

Trusting God is a key element to experiencing his
guidance. This means having confidence that where
you've been, where you are, and where you're headed

are all a part of God's plan. Trusting God also means trusting his directions, even when you've never seen the destination. If you were to see too much of your future, you might become afraid of some hard times ahead or overconfident about your accomplishments. In either case, you might be tempted to stop trusting God's guidance and wisdom for your life. God's guidance is like a flashlight that lights up just enough of the path ahead to show you where to take the next few steps. By guiding you step-by-step, God's plan is revealed in his time. He unfolds the joys and sorrows of life in doses you can handle. Each day's circumstances then become proof that God has your best interests in mind. God has a definite plan for you. He wants you to trust him to guide you each step of the way.

DIVINE PROMISE

THE LORD IS GOOD AND DOES WHAT IS RIGHT;
HE SHOWS THE PROPER PATH TO THOSE
WHO GO ASTRAY. HE LEADS THE HUMBLE IN
DOING RIGHT, TEACHING THEM HIS WAY.
THE LORD LEADS WITH UNFAILING LOVE AND
FAITHFULNESS ALL WHO KEEP HIS COVENANT
AND OBEY HIS DEMANDS. *Psalm 25:8-10*

Habits

MY QUESTIONS *for* GOD

Why do I seem to continue in bad habits? How can I break the cycle?

A Moment *with* God

Those who are dominated by the sinful nature think about sinful things, but those who are controlled by the Holy Spirit think about things that please the Spirit. So letting your sinful nature control your mind leads to death. But letting the Spirit control your mind leads to life and peace.   ROMANS 8:5-6

Do not let sin control the way you live; do not give in to sinful desires. Do not let any part of your body become an instrument of evil to serve sin. Instead, give yourselves completely to God, for you were dead, but now you have new life. So use your whole body as an instrument to do what is right for the glory of God. Sin is no longer your master, for you no longer live under the requirements of the law. Instead, you live under the freedom of God's grace.

ROMANS 6:12-14

If any of you wants to be my follower, you must turn from your selfish ways, take up your cross, and follow me. If you try to hang on to your life, you will lose it. But if you give up your life for my sake, you will save it.   MATTHEW 16:24-25

*O*ne of the biggest lies the world tells you is that you are a victim who has no power to resist the temptations around you. Our culture teaches that heredity, environment, or circumstances excuse you from responsibility. This no-fault policy actually leaves you more vulnerable to being captive to your sinful desires. But

God is more powerful than anything else that might seem to control you. When you try to control your own life, you usually end up losing control to other things. Wrong desires can easily sneak in and set up a routine of bad habits. Changing those habits isn't a matter of taking back control yourself but of giving up control to God. You may feel like your bad habits control you now, but your relationship with God gives you access to his transforming power. When you ask for God's help through prayer and seek the support of other believers, God breaks the chains that hold you and sets you free from the control of bad habits.

DIVINE PROMISE

MAKE EVERY EFFORT TO RESPOND TO GOD'S PROMISES. SUPPLEMENT YOUR FAITH WITH A GENEROUS PROVISION OF MORAL EXCELLENCE, AND MORAL EXCELLENCE WITH KNOWLEDGE, AND KNOWLEDGE WITH SELF-CONTROL, AND SELF-CONTROL WITH PATIENT ENDURANCE, AND PATIENT ENDURANCE WITH GODLINESS.

2 Peter 1:5-6

Hand of God

MY QUESTION *for* GOD

How can I learn to see the hand of God at work in my life?

A Moment *with* God

Come and see what our God has done, what awesome miracles he performs for people! PSALM 66:5

It is the LORD who provides the sun to light the day and the moon and stars to light the night, and who stirs the sea into roaring waves. His name is the LORD of Heaven's Armies. JEREMIAH 31:35

Job replied, " . . . Should we accept only good things from the hand of God and never anything bad?"

JOB 2:10

Sometimes God demonstrates his power through visible, miraculous signs. At other times the evidence of his power is much more subtle, such as when he works in your heart. Sometimes God works through events in your life or uses unlikely people to accomplish his will. Sometimes God speaks to you in a still, quiet voice in your mind, and at other times he is a force to be reckoned with. The point is that some things about God are constant and unchanging (his love, his law, his promises), but other things about God are wild and mysterious. He rarely works the same way twice, which means you need to be diligent in trusting him and continually expectant to discover how he wants to work through you next. Often it isn't until you look back on your life that you can see God's fingerprints all over it. Trust God and watch for the ways he works. These will be divine moments to be thankful that God's hand is on you now and forever.

DIVINE PROMISE

WHATEVER IS GOOD AND PERFECT COMES
DOWN TO US FROM GOD OUR FATHER, WHO
CREATED ALL THE LIGHTS IN THE HEAVENS.

James 1:17

Hard-Heartedness

MY QUESTION *for* GOD

What are the signs of a hard heart?

A MOMENT *with* GOD

Pharaoh's heart, however, remained hard. He still
refused to listen, just as the LORD had predicted.

EXODUS 7:13

The older brother was angry and wouldn't go in.
His father came out and begged him, but he replied,
"All these years I've slaved for you and never once
refused to do a single thing you told me to. And
in all that time you never gave me even one young
goat for a feast with my friends. Yet when this son
of yours comes back after squandering your money
on prostitutes, you celebrate by killing the fattened
calf!" His father said to him, "Look, dear son, you
have always stayed by me, and everything I have is
yours. We had to celebrate this happy day. For your
brother was dead and has come back to life! He was
lost, but now he is found!"   LUKE 15:28-32

"Oh no, sir!" [Hannah] replied. "I haven't been drinking wine or anything stronger. But I am very discouraged, and I was pouring out my heart to the LORD."

1 SAMUEL 1:15

$\mathscr{P}$haraoh had a hard, stubborn heart. No matter how much he heard about God or how many miracles he saw, he refused to believe. The older brother of the prodigal son also struggled with a hard heart; he was more eager to punish than forgive. Hannah, however, continued to pray to God even when nothing seemed to happen. As you evaluate the condition of your heart, you must regularly ask yourself if it is becoming hard and stubborn or open and pliable, trusting God whatever your circumstances are. If you find it hard to forgive others or if you struggle to see God at work in your daily life, then your heart may be in danger of becoming hard. If you let the process continue, you cut yourself off from God, the only one who can help you. A hard heart rejects the only thing that can save it—God's love. A soft heart is open to God's help and sees his perfectly timed responses.

DIVINE PROMISE

I WILL GIVE YOU A NEW HEART, AND I WILL PUT A NEW SPIRIT IN YOU. I WILL TAKE OUT YOUR STONY, STUBBORN HEART AND GIVE YOU A TENDER, RESPONSIVE HEART. *Ezekiel 36:26*

Health

MY QUESTION *for* GOD

How can obedience to God make me healthier?

A MOMENT *with* GOD

You and your children and grandchildren must fear
the LORD your God as long as you live. If you obey all
his decrees and commands, you will enjoy a long life.

DEUTERONOMY 6:2

I will never forget your commandments, for by them
you give me life.   PSALM 119:93

The LORD will guide you continually, giving you
water when you are dry and restoring your strength.
You will be like a well-watered garden, like an ever-
flowing spring.   ISAIAH 58:11

*O*bedience to God keeps you strong in your faith and
headed for eternal life, which is the ultimate prescription
for healthy living! Even in this life on earth, obedience to
God has health benefits. While the specific promise from
God in Deuteronomy 6:2 applied directly to the Israel-
ite nation, the verse clearly communicates the principle
that living a life of obedience to God is healthy because
God's Word tells you how to avoid habits and behaviors
that are harmful to your body. Sickness and disease are
sometimes the result of choosing to go against God's
Word (alcoholism or sexually transmitted diseases, for
example). The path of obedience to God will always take

you in a healthy direction. Some of God's most amazing blessings—strong faith, peace of heart and mind, the security of knowing him—are the results of a life of steady obedience.

DIVINE PROMISE

PHYSICAL TRAINING IS GOOD, BUT TRAINING FOR GODLINESS IS MUCH BETTER, PROMISING BENEFITS IN THIS LIFE AND IN THE LIFE TO COME. *1 Timothy 4:8*

Heaven

MY QUESTION *for* GOD

How should my hope of heaven affect my life now?

A MOMENT *with* GOD

Our present troubles are small and won't last very long. Yet they produce for us a glory that vastly outweighs them and will last forever!

2 CORINTHIANS 4:17

God has made everything beautiful for its own time. He has planted eternity in the human heart.

ECCLESIASTES 3:11

This world is not our permanent home; we are looking forward to a home yet to come. HEBREWS 13:14

As a heaven-bound follower of God, try to put heaven and earth in perspective. Here, you will probably live for less than a hundred years. In heaven, one hundred *million* years will be just the beginning! Yet God has determined that how you live during your short time on earth will prepare you for heaven. This gives you purpose in your life, perspective on your troubles, and anticipation for what God has planned for you in eternity.

Divine Promise

OUR PRESENT TROUBLES ARE SMALL AND WON'T LAST VERY LONG. YET THEY PRODUCE FOR US A GLORY THAT VASTLY OUTWEIGHS THEM AND WILL LAST FOREVER!   *2 Corinthians 4:17*

Help

My Question *for* God

How will God help me in my times of trouble?

A Moment *with* God

When you go through deep waters, I will be with you. When you go through rivers of difficulty, you will not drown. When you walk through the fire of oppression, you will not be burned up; the flames will not consume you.   Isaiah 43:2

The Lord helps the fallen and lifts those bent beneath their loads.   Psalm 145:14

When things are going badly, do you wonder, *Where is God when I need him most?* The answer is always the same—he is right beside you. God is there, and he has the power and the desire to help you. In this life God doesn't promise to save you from trouble. In fact, the Bible assures you that trouble will come your way. It's the natural consequence of living in a fallen, sinful world. God isn't like a genie in a bottle, granting your every wish; if he were, you would follow him for the wrong reasons, and your faith would never grow. Instead of preventing or removing the hard times, God helps you through them. He promises to give you wisdom to cope, strength to endure, and discernment to deal with and overcome adversity. It is through God's help today that you will learn to rely on him in the future.

DIVINE PROMISE

I WILL KEEP ON HOPING FOR YOUR HELP;
I WILL PRAISE YOU MORE AND MORE.   *Psalm 71:14*

Holy Spirit

MY QUESTION *for* GOD

How does the presence of God's Spirit make a difference in my life?

A MOMENT *with* GOD

We have received God's Spirit (not the world's
spirit), so we can know the wonderful things God has
freely given us.   1 CORINTHIANS 2:12

*T*he Holy Spirit helps you understand the deep truths
of God. The Spirit is God's presence that lives within
you, helping you discover the mysteries and wonders
of his character.

Let the Holy Spirit guide your lives. Then you won't
be doing what your sinful nature craves. The sinful
nature wants to do evil, which is just the opposite of
what the Spirit wants. And the Spirit gives us desires
that are the opposite of what the sinful nature desires.
These two forces are constantly fighting each other,
so you are not free to carry out your good intentions.

GALATIANS 5:16-17

*T*he Holy Spirit helps you know the truth about sin
and convicts you when you do sin. This is one way God
helps you distinguish between right and wrong, good
and bad, his way and the way of the world. God cares
enough about you to give you one-on-one instructions
for how to live a life that pleases him.

The Holy Spirit helps us in our weakness. For
example, we don't know what God wants us to pray
for. But the Holy Spirit prays for us with groanings
that cannot be expressed in words. And the Father

who knows all hearts knows what the Spirit is saying, for the Spirit pleads for us believers in harmony with God's own will. ROMANS 8:26-27

The Holy Spirit helps you pray. So often we long for recognition and understanding, yet we can't find the words. You can take great comfort and confidence in the fact that your prayers are heard, understood, and responded to. The Holy Spirit knows your deepest longings and expresses them to God on your behalf.

DIVINE PROMISE

THE SPIRIT IS GOD'S GUARANTEE THAT HE WILL GIVE US THE INHERITANCE HE PROMISED AND THAT HE HAS PURCHASED US TO BE HIS OWN PEOPLE. HE DID THIS SO WE WOULD PRAISE AND GLORIFY HIM. *Ephesians 1:14*

Honesty

MY QUESTION *for* GOD

How does honesty help prepare me for God's purposes?

A MOMENT *with* GOD

All who cheat with dishonest weights and measures are detestable to the LORD your God.

DEUTERONOMY 25:16

The LORD detests double standards; he is not pleased by dishonest scales.   PROVERBS 20:23

The LORD demands accurate scales and balances; he sets the standards for fairness.   PROVERBS 16:11

If you are faithful in little things, you will be faithful in large ones. But if you are dishonest in little things, you won't be honest with greater responsibilities.

                                                          LUKE 16:10

*H*onesty matters greatly to God because it reveals your character. If you're in the habit of cheating in little things, it will be very difficult to be honest when bigger challenges with bigger stakes come your way. It doesn't matter if no one else is watching—God is. Even if no one else knows, God knows. He sees your true character, which is revealed in those moments when you think no one is looking. If you can't be trusted to be honest in a small matter, you can't be trusted to be honest in a big matter. Honesty prepares you for responsibility. When you build your life with the bricks of honesty, you will have a strong foundation to act with integrity when great challenges and responsibilities come your way. When your life is governed by God's standards of fairness and justice, you'll be ready to carry out God's purposes for your life.

DIVINE PROMISE

WHO MAY CLIMB THE MOUNTAIN OF THE
LORD? WHO MAY STAND IN HIS HOLY PLACE?
ONLY THOSE WHOSE HANDS AND HEARTS ARE
PURE, WHO DO NOT WORSHIP IDOLS AND
NEVER TELL LIES. THEY WILL RECEIVE THE LORD'S
BLESSING AND HAVE A RIGHT RELATIONSHIP
WITH GOD THEIR SAVIOR.   *Psalm 24:3-5*

Hope

MY QUESTION *for* GOD

What am I supposed to be hoping for?

A MOMENT *with* GOD

All praise to God, the Father of our Lord Jesus
Christ. It is by his great mercy that we have been
born again, because God raised Jesus Christ from the
dead. Now we live with great expectation, and we
have a priceless inheritance—an inheritance that is
kept in heaven for you, pure and undefiled, beyond
the reach of change and decay. And through your
faith, God is protecting you by his power until you
receive this salvation, which is ready to be revealed
on the last day for all to see. So be truly glad. There is
wonderful joy ahead, even though you have to endure
many trials for a little while.   1 PETER 1:3-6

"I know the plans I have for you," says the LORD.
"They are plans for good and not for disaster, to give
you a future and a hope."
                                                    JEREMIAH 29:11

For a prisoner on death row, a pardon offers the hope of freedom. For the spiritual prisoner destined for eternal death because of the consequences of sin, God offers ultimate hope. He forgives your sins so that you can be with him in heaven forever. When it seems impossible to go on in life, God brings eternal hope. Hope is essential to your perseverance to get through the tough times. Without hope, you would give up. Just as focusing on a fixed point in the distance helps you travel in a straighter line, fixing your eyes on the eternal horizon helps you reach your ultimate destination of heaven. There you will live with God forever, and there will be no more pain or sorrow or suffering. As you move straight toward your eternal goal, your hope for eternity will help you endure the discomforts of daily life.

DIVINE PROMISE

O LORD, YOU ALONE ARE MY HOPE. *Psalm 71:5*

Humility

MY QUESTION *for* GOD

Why does God value a humble spirit?

A MOMENT *with* GOD

He gives us even more grace to stand against such evil desires. As the Scriptures say, "God opposes the

proud but favors the humble." So humble yourselves
before God. Resist the devil, and he will flee from
you. Come close to God, and God will come close
to you. Wash your hands, you sinners; purify your
hearts, for your loyalty is divided between God and
the world. Let there be tears for what you have done.
. . . Humble yourselves before the Lord, and he will
lift you up in honor.   JAMES 4:6-10

*H*umility is essential for recognizing the sin in your
life. Whereas pride gives the devil the key to your
heart, humility gives God your whole heart. This kind
of humility comes from godly sorrow over sin. Openly
admitting that you need God and seeking his forgiveness is something that no proud person can do. When
you give your whole heart to God, you open yourself
up to be used for his purposes in all times and places!

DIVINE PROMISE

HUMBLE YOURSELVES UNDER THE MIGHTY
POWER OF GOD, AND AT THE RIGHT TIME HE
WILL LIFT YOU UP IN HONOR.   *1 Peter 5:6*

Hurts

MY QUESTION *for* GOD

How does God want me to respond to those who hurt me?

A Moment *with* God

Peter came to him and asked, "Lord, how often should I forgive someone who sins against me? Seven times?" "No, not seven times," Jesus replied, "but seventy times seven!"   MATTHEW 18:21-22

Since God chose you to be the holy people he loves, you must clothe yourselves with tenderhearted mercy, kindness, humility, gentleness, and patience. Make allowance for each other's faults, and forgive anyone who offends you. Remember, the Lord forgave you, so you must forgive others.

COLOSSIANS 3:12-13

When God forgives, he wipes away the past and forgets it, so you should not remember it either. God's forgiveness deletes the sin file from the hard drive of your heart. When dealing with people who have hurt you, the only thing within your control is the choice to forgive them. Ask God to help you do this. Forgiveness removes the bitterness from your soul and begins to heal the hurt. Remember that your own sin has deeply hurt God, yet he forgives you and restores his relationship with you. You should follow his example or else live with a bitter spirit. Your hurts matter to God, but it is only by forgiving those who have hurt you that you can be free to experience God's comfort and peace of mind.

DIVINE PROMISE

IF YOU FORGIVE THOSE WHO SIN AGAINST YOU, YOUR HEAVENLY FATHER WILL FORGIVE YOU.
Matthew 6:14

Impact

MY QUESTION *for* GOD

How can I, as a Christian, have the greatest impact on my friends?

A MOMENT *with* GOD

You must worship Christ as Lord of your life. And if someone asks about your Christian hope, always be ready to explain it. But do this in a gentle and respectful way. Keep your conscience clear. Then if people speak against you, they will be ashamed when they see what a good life you live because you belong to Christ. 1 PETER 3:15-16

Owe nothing to anyone—except for your obligation to love one another. ROMANS 13:8

God's influence in your life is attractive to others. The more you reflect God's perfect character, the more people will be drawn to you and want to be around you. Make it your goal that your friends and classmates are able to say, "We can plainly see that God is with you." Can others say that about you right now? When they do, it's a divine moment for them and for you.

DIVINE PROMISE

YOU ARE THE LIGHT OF THE WORLD. . . . NO ONE LIGHTS A LAMP AND THEN PUTS IT UNDER A BASKET. INSTEAD, A LAMP IS PLACED ON A STAND, WHERE IT GIVES LIGHT TO EVERYONE IN THE HOUSE. IN THE SAME WAY, LET YOUR GOOD DEEDS SHINE OUT FOR ALL TO SEE, SO THAT EVERYONE WILL PRAISE YOUR HEAVENLY FATHER.   *Matthew 5:14-16*

Impossible

MY QUESTION *for* GOD

Can God do the impossible for me?

A MOMENT *with* GOD

He rescues and saves his people; he performs miraculous signs and wonders in the heavens and on earth. He has rescued Daniel from the power of the lions.   DANIEL 6:27

Those who heard this said, "Then who in the world can be saved?" [Jesus] replied, "What is impossible for people is possible with God."   LUKE 18:26-27

Then Abraham bowed down to the ground, but he laughed to himself in disbelief. "How could I become a father at the age of 100?" he thought. "And how can Sarah have a baby when she is ninety years old?" . . . Then the LORD said . . . "Is anything too hard for the LORD? I will return about this time next year, and Sarah will have a son."   GENESIS 17:17; 18:13-14

The LORD kept his word and did for Sarah exactly what he had promised. She became pregnant, and she gave birth to a son for Abraham in his old age. This happened at just the time God had said it would.

GENESIS 21:1-2

This is what the LORD of Heaven's Armies says: "All this may seem impossible to you now, a small remnant of God's people. But is it impossible for me?" says the LORD of Heaven's Armies.   ZECHARIAH 8:6

The Bible is filled with stories of the impossible: A flood covers the earth, a sea is parted so people can walk through it, the sun keeps shining until a battle can be won, a man survives three days in the belly of a fish, a virgin gives birth to a baby boy. To the person who does not believe in God or the authority of the Bible, these stories defy logic. But those who believe in the Creator of all things also believe that he can alter what he has created; he can break natural law to cause something supernatural to happen. In order to experience the impossible and recognize it for what it is, you need faith. Faith opens up a new dimension so you can understand that what you see with your eyes is not all there is. You can recognize the "impossible" things God does for his people because you believe that anything is possible for him. Learn to recognize and appreciate the impossible things God accomplishes for you and around you each day: the gift of forgiveness, the change of seasons, the intricacies of the human body and its ability to heal, the exact conditions needed to support life on this earth, the birth of a baby. The more you see the impossible acts of God with eyes of faith, the stronger your faith in God will become. There should be no doubt that God specializes in doing what, from a human perspective, is impossible. But the end of your abilities is the beginning of his. The God who spoke all creation into being can do the impossible for you. Simply believe that he can—and that he wants to.

DIVINE PROMISE

NOW ALL GLORY TO GOD, WHO IS ABLE, THROUGH HIS MIGHTY POWER AT WORK WITHIN US, TO ACCOMPLISH INFINITELY MORE THAN WE MIGHT ASK OR THINK. *Ephesians 3:20*

Influence

MY QUESTION *for* GOD

How can I know if my life counts for Jesus?

A MOMENT *with* GOD

After all, who is Apollos? Who is Paul? We are only God's servants through whom you believed the

Good News. Each of us did the work the Lord gave us. I planted the seed in your hearts, and Apollos watered it, but it was God who made it grow. It's not important who does the planting, or who does the watering. What's important is that God makes the seed grow. The one who plants and the one who waters work together with the same purpose. And both will be rewarded for their own hard work.

1 CORINTHIANS 3:5-8

*O*n this side of eternity, you may not be able to see how your life influences others. But you may be planting seeds of faith in the lives of people around you, seeds that God will care for and nourish until they grow into a saving relationship with him. Instead of trying too hard to influence people, live every day, moment by moment, in obedience to God. Years of living in daily obedience develop the character and integrity that draw others to Jesus.

DIVINE PROMISE

WE KNOW, DEAR BROTHERS AND SISTERS, THAT GOD LOVES YOU AND HAS CHOSEN YOU TO BE HIS OWN PEOPLE. FOR WHEN WE BROUGHT YOU THE GOOD NEWS, IT WAS NOT ONLY WITH WORDS BUT ALSO WITH POWER, FOR THE HOLY SPIRIT GAVE YOU FULL ASSURANCE THAT WHAT WE SAID WAS TRUE. AND YOU KNOW OF OUR CONCERN FOR YOU FROM THE WAY WE LIVED WHEN WE WERE WITH YOU. *1 Thessalonians 1:4-5*

Insecurity

MY QUESTION for GOD

How can I overcome the insecurities that get in the way of my being used by God?

A MOMENT with GOD

We are God's masterpiece. He has created us anew in Christ Jesus, so we can do the good things he planned for us long ago.   EPHESIANS 2:10

You have not received a spirit that makes you fearful slaves. Instead, you received God's Spirit when he adopted you as his own children. Now we call him, "Abba, Father." For his Spirit joins with our spirit to affirm that we are God's children.   ROMANS 8:15-16

God made you in his own image, so he must value you highly! He doesn't make mistakes; he created you with unique gifts so you can do the specific tasks he has for you. He does not expect more from you than what he knows you can give, but he does expect you to use what he has given you. That is why it is so important to discover your own special God-given gifts. When you find the right area of service to use your unique gifts, you will have a match made in heaven. Your insecurities will melt away, and you will become bold in serving God. Your hesitancy will turn into divine moments of joy and passion.

DIVINE PROMISE

I CAN DO EVERYTHING THROUGH CHRIST, WHO GIVES ME STRENGTH. *Philippians 4:13*

Insignificance

MY QUESTION *for* GOD

I feel like my life is so small and insignificant. How can I make it count for God?

A MOMENT *with* GOD

My life is worth nothing to me unless I use it for finishing the work assigned me by the Lord Jesus— the work of telling others the Good News about the wonderful grace of God.   ACTS 20:24

Do not despise these small beginnings, for the LORD rejoices to see the work begin.   ZECHARIAH 4:10

Deep within every human heart is the longing for significance. We want our life to count, to make a difference, to be worth something. Everywhere we look, we see others who are more successful, more gifted, more this, more that. No wonder so many of us feel insignificant! You're not the only one who struggles with these feelings. Many people think they're not doing anything truly important or really making a difference. And many people spend far more time paralyzed by what they cannot do than acting on what they can do; their inabilities overshadow their abilities. But one of the great lessons of the Bible is that the heroes of the faith—people like Moses, Gideon, Esther, and Peter—were ordinary people who learned that their significance came not from what *they* could accomplish with their abilities, but from what *God* could accomplish through their abilities. Significance comes from knowing you are a unique creation of almighty God, who has given you specific abilities he wants you to use for a bigger purpose. When you use your God-given abilities to accomplish his work, your life becomes significant both now and for eternity.

Divine Promise

REMEMBER, DEAR BROTHERS AND SISTERS, THAT FEW OF YOU WERE WISE IN THE WORLD'S EYES OR POWERFUL OR WEALTHY WHEN GOD CALLED YOU.   *1 Corinthians 1:26*

Integrity

My Question *for* God

What does it mean to live with integrity?

A Moment *with* God

If you are faithful in little things, you will be faithful in large ones. But if you are dishonest in little things, you won't be honest with greater responsibilities.

LUKE 16:10

[Pilate] announced his verdict. "You brought this man to me, accusing him of leading a revolt. I have examined him thoroughly on this point in your presence and find him innocent. Herod came to the same conclusion and sent him back to us. Nothing this man has done calls for the death penalty." LUKE 23:14-15

*L*iving with integrity means there is consistency between your beliefs, your character, and your actions. Integrity means you know what you believe and live as though you believe it. You build integrity over time as you consistently demonstrate honest dependability through your words and your actions. No one is a better model of this than Jesus. Though you can never be perfect, as he was, you can always grow in integrity. This involves being faithful in every area of your life, no matter how small. In fact, you'll probably find that it is in the small things that your integrity is tested the most. When you are tested, remember that each one of your actions has consequences. What you do every day is forging your reputation. Your momentary actions are developing the qualities by which you will long be remembered. Eventually you may find yourself in a situation where your integrity is the only thing you have left. Because of your integrity, people will trust you and look up to you. The right thing will be done, and you will be able to thank God that your integrity created a divine moment.

Divine Promise

TO THE FAITHFUL YOU SHOW YOURSELF FAITHFUL; TO THOSE WITH INTEGRITY YOU SHOW INTEGRITY.   *2 Samuel 22:26*

Invitation

My Question *for* God

How does Jesus invite me to experience him?

A Moment *with* God

Jesus called out to them, "Come, follow me, and I will show you how to fish for people!" And they left their nets at once and followed him.   Matthew 4:19-20

*J*esus' invitation to follow him remains a mere opportunity until you decide to accept it. If Peter and Andrew had responded to Jesus' call by saying, "That's a very interesting invitation—maybe we can talk about it again after fishing season," they would not have become Jesus' disciples. Jesus' invitation demands a decision: Follow him or remain where you are. Accepting his invitation leads to action; the disciples left their nets and followed Jesus. God has extended his invitation to you, too. Have you given him your RSVP, "Accepted with gratitude"?

DIVINE PROMISE

GOD WILL DO THIS, FOR HE IS FAITHFUL TO
DO WHAT HE SAYS, AND HE HAS INVITED
YOU INTO PARTNERSHIP WITH HIS SON, JESUS
CHRIST OUR LORD. *1 Corinthians 1:9*

Involvement

MY QUESTION *for* GOD

How involved do I need to be in helping others?

A MOMENT *with* GOD

If you see your neighbor's ox or sheep or goat
wandering away, don't ignore your responsibility.
Take it back to its owner. . . . Do the same if you find
your neighbor's donkey, clothing, or anything else
your neighbor loses. DEUTERONOMY 22:1-3

Be careful to live properly among your unbelieving
neighbors. Then even if they accuse you of doing
wrong, they will see your honorable behavior,
and they will give honor to God when he judges
the world. 1 PETER 2:12

Live wisely among those who are not believers,
and make the most of every opportunity. Let your
conversation be gracious and attractive so that you
will have the right response for everyone.

COLOSSIANS 4:5-6

In our world we seem to find it increasingly easy to say, "I don't want to get involved." Maybe our excuse is that the situation looks too messy or complicated. Sometimes people are even sued for trying to help someone else. When you see someone in need or notice something you could do to help, you may be tempted to turn a blind eye and pretend you don't notice. You may hope someone else will do something about it. God reminds us that we are to be compassionate and active, ready and willing to go the extra mile to be good neighbors. God's command to love your neighbor is a command to take action. He doesn't say to love your neighbor when it's convenient—he says make the most of *every* opportunity. In today's "mind your own business" culture, having the courage to get involved certainly gets attention. Opportunities to get involved are also God's way of getting your attention. When you get involved by helping someone, you may have a divine moment or bring a divine moment to that person. One of the best ways to experience God is to get involved in the lives of others!

DIVINE CHALLENGE

NOW I AM GIVING YOU A NEW COMMANDMENT: LOVE EACH OTHER. JUST AS I HAVE LOVED YOU, YOU SHOULD LOVE EACH OTHER. YOUR LOVE FOR ONE ANOTHER WILL PROVE TO THE WORLD THAT YOU ARE MY DISCIPLES. *John 13:34-35*

Joy

MY QUESTION *for* GOD

How can I find lasting joy despite life's ups and downs?

A MOMENT *with* GOD

Always be full of joy in the Lord. I say it again—
rejoice! Let everyone see that you are considerate
in all you do.   PHILIPPIANS 4:4-5

I have learned how to be content with whatever I
have. I know how to live on almost nothing or with
everything. I have learned the secret of living in every
situation, whether it is with a full stomach or empty,
with plenty or little.   PHILIPPIANS 4:11-12

You are an emotional being because God created
you to have feelings. It is not unusual or abnormal to
experience emotional or spiritual highs and lows within
short periods of time. However, lasting joy and contentment run much deeper than the emotions of the moment. This kind of joy is like a strong current that runs
deep beneath the stormy surface of your feelings. Joy is
the celebration of walking with God. It is the sense of
security that comes only from being held by an almighty
God. It is the peace of knowing that God accepts you
for who you are and wants you to be with him forever
in eternity. It is the quiet confidence you experience
when you let God guide you at all times and in all things,
knowing that wherever he guides you, it is in your best

interests. No emotional ups and downs can shake that kind of strong foundation.

DIVINE PROMISE

LET THE GODLY REJOICE. LET THEM BE GLAD IN GOD'S PRESENCE. LET THEM BE FILLED WITH JOY.   *Psalm 68:3*

Judging Others

MY QUESTION *for* GOD

What's the difference between constructive criticism and judging others?

A MOMENT *with* GOD

Do not judge others, and you will not be judged. For you will be treated as you treat others. The standard you use in judging is the standard by which you will be judged. And why worry about a speck in your friend's eye when you have a log in your own?

MATTHEW 7:1-3

Don't speak evil against each other, dear brothers and sisters. If you criticize and judge each other, then you are criticizing and judging God's law. But your job is to obey the law, not to judge whether it applies to you.

JAMES 4:11

*O*ne coach berates a player publicly for making a mistake in a game. Another coach waits until the game is over and privately tells the player how to avoid making the same mistake again. Though no one likes criticism—even when it is constructive—we sometimes need it. It is much easier to receive criticism when it is offered gently and in love rather than in a harsh or humiliating way. To judge others is to criticize with no intent of seeing them succeed or improve. To offer constructive criticism is to have the goal of building a relationship and helping them become who God created them to be. Judging others is hurtful, and it helps no one. Constructive criticism can bring a divine moment of change.

DIVINE PROMISE

MAKE ALLOWANCE FOR EACH OTHER'S FAULTS, AND FORGIVE ANYONE WHO OFFENDS YOU. REMEMBER, THE LORD FORGAVE YOU, SO YOU MUST FORGIVE OTHERS. *Colossians 3:13*

Knowledge and Learning

MY QUESTION *for* GOD

How can I recognize God in my learning experiences?

A MOMENT *with* GOD

Get wisdom; develop good judgment. Don't forget my words or turn away from them.   PROVERBS 4:5

Take a lesson from the ants, you lazybones. Learn from their ways and become wise! PROVERBS 6:6

To learn, you must love discipline. PROVERBS 12:1

Then, as I looked and thought about it, I learned this lesson. PROVERBS 24:32

Keep putting into practice all you learned.

PHILIPPIANS 4:9

You didn't choose me. I chose you. I appointed you to go and produce lasting fruit, so that the Father will give you whatever you ask for, using my name.

JOHN 15:16

The things you learn and the knowledge you gain can become powerful means for God to carry out his plans through you. What you learn at school can help you do God's work because it gives you greater insight into how God's world works. Sometimes you don't like what you're studying or you aren't interested in a particular subject, but have you ever considered that you're in that class for a reason? If you've never thought about school as a place where you can learn about God, think again! The knowledge you gain at school might be God's way of preparing you for something in your future, something you have yet to discover. God will use your knowledge and learning experiences for a unique purpose. If you've been blessed with the opportunity to get an education, take advantage of it. God will use it to make you even more fruitful for him. Have you

been blessed with certain skills or talents? Thank God
for them, and use them to serve him. God chose you
and created you for a purpose, and that can be exciting
even if you're studying subjects you dislike. Often God
shows you what to do as you make use of the opportunities—and classes—he sends your way. Make the
most of where you are right now so you can make the
most of where God will place you in the future.

DIVINE PROMISE

CRY OUT FOR INSIGHT, AND ASK FOR
UNDERSTANDING. SEARCH FOR THEM. . . .
THEN YOU WILL UNDERSTAND WHAT IT MEANS
TO FEAR THE LORD, AND YOU WILL GAIN
KNOWLEDGE OF GOD.   *Proverbs 2:3-5*

Limitations

MY QUESTION *for* GOD

*What does God think when he sees all my faults
and limitations?*

A MOMENT *with* GOD

The angel of the LORD came and sat beneath the great
tree at Ophrah, which belonged to Joash of the clan
of Abiezer. Gideon son of Joash was threshing wheat
at the bottom of a winepress to hide the grain from
the Midianites. The angel of the LORD appeared to
him and said, "Mighty hero, the LORD is with you!"

. . . "But Lord," Gideon replied, "how can I rescue Israel? My clan is the weakest in the whole tribe of Manasseh, and I am the least in my entire family!"

JUDGES 6:11-12, 15

The angel of the Lord greeted Gideon by calling him "mighty hero." Was God talking to the right person? This was Gideon—the guy who was hiding in a winepress from his enemies, the guy who claimed he was the least of his family. Yet God called him a mighty hero. God's message to Gideon—and to you—is clear: You are more than what you appear to be or what you think you are. God calls out the best in you. He sees more in you than you see in yourself. You may look at your limitations, but God looks at your potential. If you want to increase your opportunities, learn to see life from God's perspective. He doesn't put nearly as many limitations on you as you put on yourself. He sees within you the person he created you to be. How encouraging—the almighty God of the universe sees you for what you can become rather than for what you are! Don't hide because of your limitations; allow God to give you a divine moment by using you in spite of them.

DIVINE PROMISE

GLORY TO GOD, WHO IS ABLE, THROUGH HIS MIGHTY POWER AT WORK WITHIN US, TO ACCOMPLISH INFINITELY MORE THAN WE MIGHT ASK OR THINK. *Ephesians 3:20*

Listening

MY QUESTION *for* GOD

How can I better listen to God?

A MOMENT *with* GOD

Each morning I bring my requests to you and wait
expectantly.   PSALM 5:3

Be still, and know that I am God!   PSALM 46:10

So pay attention to how you hear. To those who listen
to my teaching, more understanding will be given.
But for those who are not listening, even what they
think they understand will be taken away from them.

LUKE 8:18

God speaks to you in many ways, but you must pay attention to what he is saying. One way to listen to God is
to schedule quiet time with him each day. Use this special time to be still before him and wait expectantly for
him to speak. God often speaks to you as you pray and
read his Word. God can also speak to you unexpectedly
through the words of a close friend, the instruction of
a wise teacher, or the beauty of a sunset or a moving
song. Pay attention to the many ways God is speaking
to you, and carve out times you can devote to listening
to him. Don't miss an opportunity for a lesson from the
master Teacher. The more you listen to God, the more
you will hear him.

DIVINE PROMISE

COME AND LISTEN TO MY COUNSEL. I'LL SHARE
MY HEART WITH YOU AND MAKE YOU WISE.
Proverbs 1:23

Listening

MY QUESTION *for* GOD

How can I be sure that God is listening to my prayers?

A MOMENT *with* GOD

The eyes of the Lord watch over those who do right,
and his ears are open to their prayers.   1 PETER 3:12

The LORD is far from the wicked, but he hears the
prayers of the righteous.   PROVERBS 15:29

Devote yourselves to prayer with an alert mind and a
thankful heart.   COLOSSIANS 4:2

Sometimes you may feel as if your prayers are bouncing
off the ceiling. You wonder, *Is God paying any attention?*
The bigger question is, are you paying attention to God's
response? God always answers prayer. He does so because he is loving and good. It's his nature to give good
things to his people. After the things you pray about
work out, sometimes you may fail to give God the credit
because you didn't notice that he answered! When you
pray, be alert and watch for God's response, even if it
isn't what you wanted. Then don't forget to thank him

for his answer, no matter what it is, because you can be confident that it is in your best interest.

DIVINE PROMISE

YOU CAN BE SURE OF THIS: THE LORD SET APART THE GODLY FOR HIMSELF. THE LORD WILL ANSWER WHEN I CALL TO HIM. *Psalm 4:3*

Loneliness

MY QUESTION *for* GOD

How can God help me when I feel all alone?

A MOMENT *with* GOD

I am the only one left.   1 KINGS 19:10

He went in alone and shut the door behind him and prayed to the LORD.   2 KINGS 4:33

How precious are your thoughts about me, O God. They cannot be numbered!   PSALM 139:17

*Y*ou may feel alone, but God is always with you. He is thinking about you all the time. Don't give up on God when you feel lonely. Don't abandon all relationships because a few have failed. This will only make you feel sorry for yourself and become bitter. Use "alone times" to discover the faithfulness of God. As you recognize

God's faithfulness, you will be compelled to be faithful to others, even when they abandon you. Getting involved with other people will take the focus off your lonely feelings and direct it toward someone else's well-being. Put yourself in places where you can meet and get to know other people—church is a great place to start. Soon your life will be full and blessed with friendships.

DIVINE PROMISE

THOSE WHO KNOW YOUR NAME TRUST IN YOU, FOR YOU, O LORD, DO NOT ABANDON THOSE WHO SEARCH FOR YOU.   *Psalm 9:10*

Love

MY QUESTION *for* GOD

How do I love God with all my heart, soul, and strength?

A MOMENT *with* GOD

You must love the LORD your God with all your heart, all your soul, and all your strength.

DEUTERONOMY 6:5

I love the LORD because he hears my voice and my prayer for mercy.   PSALM 116:1

When you obey my commandments, you remain in my love. . . . I have told you these things so that

you will be filled with my joy. Yes, your joy will
overflow!   JOHN 15:10-11

Your love for one another will prove to the world that
you are my disciples.   JOHN 13:35

Love covers a multitude of sins.   1 PETER 4:8

If we love each other, God lives in us, and his love is
brought to full expression in us.   1 JOHN 4:12

*I*n our culture love is usually defined in romantic
or sentimental terms. According to the Bible, love is
indeed a feeling, but it is also more than that. It is a
commitment that both protects and produces passionate feelings. Because it is a commitment, love is not
dependent on warm feelings alone but on a consistent
and courageous decision to extend yourself for the
well-being of someone else. Loving feelings can produce commitment, but commitment can also produce
loving feelings. Jesus perfectly demonstrated God's
unconditional love for you when he made the loving
commitment to lay down his life to save you from your
sins. When you love God with all your heart, soul, and
strength, you are making a commitment to develop
a relationship with the Creator of the universe, who
loved you first and daily pursues you with his love.

DIVINE PROMISE

THE LORD SAYS, "I WILL RESCUE THOSE WHO
LOVE ME. I WILL PROTECT THOSE WHO TRUST

IN MY NAME. WHEN THEY CALL ON ME, I WILL
ANSWER; I WILL BE WITH THEM IN TROUBLE.
I WILL RESCUE AND HONOR THEM. I WILL
REWARD THEM WITH A LONG LIFE AND GIVE
THEM MY SALVATION." *Psalm 91:14-16*

Love

MY QUESTION *for* GOD

How am I to love my neighbors?

A MOMENT *with* GOD

Always judge people fairly. Do not spread slanderous
gossip among your people. Do not stand idly by when
your neighbor's life is threatened. I am the LORD.

LEVITICUS 19:15-16

Now I am giving you a new commandment: Love
each other. Just as I have loved you, you should love
each other. Your love for one another will prove to
the world that you are my disciples.   JOHN 13:34-35

If we love each other, God lives in us, and his love is
brought to full expression in us.   1 JOHN 4:12

Love your neighbor as yourself.   MATTHEW 22:39

*W*hy did Jesus say to love your neighbor as yourself?
Because God knows that our first instinct is to take
care of ourselves. If we can learn to meet the needs
of others in the same way we meet our own needs,

then we will be fulfilling Jesus' command. Caring for others is what loving our neighbor is all about. Every time you show love to others, you are creating a divine moment in which God is touching two hearts—theirs and yours.

DIVINE PROMISE

IT IS GOOD WHEN YOU OBEY THE ROYAL LAW AS FOUND IN THE SCRIPTURES: "LOVE YOUR NEIGHBOR AS YOURSELF." *James 2:8*

Meaning

MY QUESTION *for* GOD

How does knowing God bring meaning to my life?

A MOMENT *with* GOD

The LORD says, "I will guide you along the best pathway for your life. I will advise you and watch over you."   PSALM 32:8

For you know that God paid a ransom to save you from the empty life you inherited from your ancestors. And the ransom he paid was not mere gold or silver.   1 PETER 1:18

Our great desire is that you will keep on loving others as long as life lasts, in order to make certain

that what you hope for will come true. Then you will
not become spiritually dull and indifferent.

HEBREWS 6:11-12

The hopes of the godly result in happiness, but the
expectations of the wicked come to nothing.

PROVERBS 10:28

*M*any people think that the Christian life is a boring
ritual of following the rules—"Don't do this," "You
can't do that." But those who discover that following
God is about relationship rather than rules are never
bored. The Christian life is full and exciting when you
realize that God loves you, he created you for a specific purpose, and he wants to work through you to
accomplish his work in the world. Think of it—the
God of the universe created you just so that he could
be your friend and do his mighty work through you.
This changes your whole outlook on life and infuses
it with meaning and purpose as you catch God's vision and direction for you. Now you can focus on using and developing your God-given gifts. You can look
forward to the eternal rewards God promises to those
who carry out his purposes. Your life will be more
meaningful and filled with divine moments in which
God guides you and encourages you. If you feel that
your life lacks meaning, perhaps it is because you are
not making yourself available to God. Ask him to help
you find your purpose in life and to pour out his blessings through you to others.

DIVINE PROMISE

THE LORD GAVE ME THIS MESSAGE: "I KNEW
YOU BEFORE I FORMED YOU IN YOUR MOTHER'S
WOMB. BEFORE YOU WERE BORN I SET
YOU APART." *Jeremiah 1:4-5*

Memories

MY QUESTION *for* GOD

*How can I overcome the memories that are keeping me in
the past?*

A MOMENT *with* GOD

Then the LORD rained down fire and burning sulfur
from the sky on Sodom and Gomorrah. He utterly
destroyed them, along with the other cities and
villages of the plain, wiping out all the people and
every bit of vegetation. But Lot's wife looked back as
she was following behind him, and she turned into a
pillar of salt.   GENESIS 19:24-26

Jesus told him, "Anyone who puts a hand to the plow
and then looks back is not fit for the Kingdom of God."

LUKE 9:62

By looking back at the smoldering cities of Sodom
and Gomorrah, Lot's wife demonstrated that she was
unwilling to turn away from her former life. It is vir-
tually impossible for you to obey God if you are still

holding on to old memories of a sinful lifestyle and longing to do the things you did before you found God. It's like trying to walk in two directions at once! If you are hanging on to sinful habits or memories from your old life, God wants you to turn completely away from them so you can experience the life he offers you. Like Lot's wife, you may be thwarting God's plans by allowing yourself to look back at the past. But when you commit yourself to looking forward, with your eyes fixed on heaven, it will truly change the way you live. It is only by looking forward to everything God has to offer—rather than looking back at what Satan offered—that you will be able to overcome the memories that keep you stuck in the past.

DIVINE PROMISE

THE KIND OF SORROW GOD WANTS US TO EXPERIENCE LEADS US AWAY FROM SIN AND RESULTS IN SALVATION. THERE'S NO REGRET FOR THAT KIND OF SORROW.   *2 Corinthians 7:10*

Mercy

MY QUESTION *for* GOD

How does God's mercy affect my daily life?

A MOMENT *with* GOD

The LORD is compassionate and merciful, slow to get angry and filled with unfailing love.   PSALM 103:8

Sin is no longer your master, for you no longer live under the requirements of the law. Instead, you live under the freedom of God's grace.   ROMANS 6:14

Let us come boldly to the throne of our gracious God. There we will receive his mercy, and we will find grace to help us when we need it most.

HEBREWS 4:16

*M*ercy is another word for the amazing kindness that God showers on you even though you do not deserve it. God's greatest act of kindness is to offer you salvation and eternal life despite the times you have ignored him, neglected him, and rebelled against him. Through forgiveness, God's mercy sets you free from the power of sin so that you can choose each day to overpower your sinful nature. God's mercy changes your life when you understand what it feels like to be loved even though you have not always shown love in return. This should cause you to love others in the same way that God loves you—by showing them mercy and thus creating a divine moment in their lives.

DIVINE PROMISE

I PROMISE THIS VERY DAY THAT I WILL REPAY TWO BLESSINGS FOR EACH OF YOUR TROUBLES.
Zechariah 9:12

Miracles

Does God still perform miracles today? How can I see more miracles in my life?

Moses and Aaron did just as the LORD had commanded them. When Aaron raised his hand and struck the ground with his staff, gnats infested the entire land, covering the Egyptians and their animals. All the dust in the land of Egypt turned into gnats. Pharaoh's magicians tried to do the same thing with their secret arts, but this time they failed. And the gnats covered everyone, people and animals alike. "This is the finger of God!" the magicians exclaimed to Pharaoh. But Pharaoh's heart remained hard. He wouldn't listen to them, just as the LORD had predicted.   EXODUS 8:17-19

God confirmed the message by giving signs and wonders and various miracles and gifts of the Holy Spirit whenever he chose.   HEBREWS 2:4

Who can list the glorious miracles of the LORD? Who can ever praise him enough?   PSALM 106:2

Come and see what our God has done, what awesome miracles he performs for people!   PSALM 66:5

The miracles of God recorded in the Bible can seem like ancient myths if you fail to recognize God's work in your life today. Pharaoh was blind to the power of God despite the miracles performed right before his eyes; you, too, can be blind to God's miracles despite the mighty works he is doing all around you. When you look for God, he will show himself in miraculous ways. Maybe you think a miracle is always a dramatic event, like raising someone from the dead. But miracles are happening all around you! These supernatural occurrences may not be as dramatic as the parting of the Red Sea, but they are no less powerful. Think of the birth of a baby, an awesome sunset, the healing of an illness, the restoration of a hopeless relationship, the rebirth of the earth in spring, salvation by faith alone, the specific call of God in your life. These are just a few incredible ways God acts in his creation. If you think you've never seen a miracle, look closer—they're happening all around you.

DIVINE PROMISE

NO PAGAN GOD IS LIKE YOU, O LORD. NONE CAN DO WHAT YOU DO! *Psalm 86:8*

MY QUESTION *for* GOD

How can I experience God by learning from my mistakes?

A MOMENT *with* GOD

I focus on this one thing: Forgetting the past and
looking forward to what lies ahead, I press on.

PHILIPPIANS 3:13-14

I am certain that God, who began the good work
within you, will continue his work until it is finally
finished on the day when Christ Jesus returns.

PHILIPPIANS 1:6

Fear of the LORD is the foundation of true wisdom.
All who obey his commandments will grow in
wisdom.   PSALM 111:10

There's a big difference between making a mistake and
committing a sin. Giving the wrong answer on a test
is a mistake; cheating in order to get a better grade is a
sin. You can often avoid repeating a mistake by studying harder, planning better, or double-checking your
work. But to avoid repeating a sin, you need God's help.
The regret you feel over sin indicates that you want to
be different——a desire that comes from God. Like sin,
even mistakes can have costly consequences, especially
if you make the same mistake over and over again. The
ability to learn from your mistakes and to develop your
character also comes from God. Through his Word,
he provides the wisdom you need to learn from your
mistakes and become mature enough to avoid making
the same mistakes again. Then when tricky situations
arise, a divine moment occurs because you know how

to respond. You see how God is helping you grow, and you avoid the mistakes and sins of your past.

DIVINE PROMISE

WE HAVE NOT STOPPED PRAYING FOR YOU SINCE WE FIRST HEARD ABOUT YOU. WE ASK GOD TO GIVE YOU COMPLETE KNOWLEDGE OF HIS WILL AND TO GIVE YOU SPIRITUAL WISDOM AND UNDERSTANDING. THEN THE WAY YOU LIVE WILL ALWAYS HONOR AND PLEASE THE LORD, AND YOUR LIVES WILL PRODUCE EVERY KIND OF GOOD FRUIT. ALL THE WHILE, YOU WILL GROW AS YOU LEARN TO KNOW GOD BETTER AND BETTER. *Colossians 1:9-10*

Motivation

MY QUESTION *for* GOD

What can motivate me in my spiritual life?

A MOMENT *with* GOD

The seed on the rocky soil represents those who hear the message and immediately receive it with joy. But since they don't have deep roots, they don't last long. They fall away as soon as they have problems.

MATTHEW 13:20-21

*S*piritual dropouts are those who have lost the enthusiasm to continue their relationship with God. A

person who lacks depth has no place for the seeds of
God's Word to grow. Without that depth, the hot sun
of persecution or problems causes their excitement to
wither. Their sense of purpose fades, and along with
it, their relationship with God. Your motivation grows
in proportion to the depth of your relationship with
God. As your relationship with him deepens, your enthusiasm for your tasks will increase. You will become
deeply rooted in God and thrive under his care and
provision in your life. The best way to find motivation
is to begin with your relationship with God.

Be very careful to obey all the commands and the
instructions that Moses gave to you. Love the LORD
your God, walk in all his ways, obey his commands,
hold firmly to him, and serve him with all your heart
and all your soul.   JOSHUA 22:5

*T*here are times when following God is serious business. But there is also great delight in knowing that the
God of the universe loves you and has a plan to use you
in a powerful way. In fact, he tells you to serve him
enthusiastically, joyfully, and with delight. God understands that enthusiasm lights the fire of service. Often
your greatest motivation comes when your actions are
compelled by love and joy.

Jesus called out to them, "Come, follow me, and I
will show you how to fish for people!"   MATTHEW 4:19

God's gifts and his call can never be withdrawn.
                                              ROMANS 11:29

*R*eclaim your sense of God's purpose for your life. You can make an impact for eternity through God's power at work within you. Working as God's partner to advance God's Kingdom—now there's something to be motivated about!

DIVINE PROMISE

RESTORE TO ME THE JOY OF YOUR SALVATION, AND MAKE ME WILLING TO OBEY YOU.

Psalm 51:12

Music

MY QUESTION *for* GOD

How does music affect the way I worship God?

A MOMENT *with* GOD

Moses and the people of Israel sang this song to the LORD: "I will sing to the LORD, for he has triumphed gloriously; he has hurled both horse and rider into the sea. The LORD is my strength and my song; he has given me victory. This is my God, and I will praise him—my father's God, and I will exalt him!

EXODUS 15:1-2

Praise the LORD! How good to sing praises to our God! How delightful and how fitting!   PSALM 147:1

The beauty and harmony of music testify to the glory and majesty of God. While the lyrics you sing direct your mind toward God, the beauty of the music touches your heart in a way that simple words cannot. It gives you a glimpse into the awesome, creative beauty of God himself. For centuries music has played an essential role in expressing our worship of God. After God rescued the Israelites from the Egyptians, his people composed a song to express their joy and gratitude to him for their deliverance. While music can be an expressive outlet of faith, it can also be a practical tool for teaching and remembering the truths of God. Music can help you worship God by accompanying the stories of his greatness. Singing hymns and songs is a testimony and expression of your gratitude and praise, helping you worship God in a meaningful way.

DIVINE PROMISE

THOSE WHO HAVE BEEN RANSOMED BY THE LORD WILL RETURN. THEY WILL ENTER JERUSALEM SINGING, CROWNED WITH EVERLASTING JOY. SORROW AND MOURNING WILL DISAPPEAR, AND THEY WILL BE FILLED WITH JOY AND GLADNESS. *Isaiah 51:11*

Mystery

My Question *for* God

Why are there mysteries and things we don't understand about God?

A Moment *with* God

Just as you cannot understand the path of the wind or the mystery of a tiny baby growing in its mother's womb, so you cannot understand the activity of God, who does all things.   ECCLESIASTES 11:5

Dear friends, we are already God's children, but he has not yet shown us what we will be like when Christ appears. But we do know that we will be like him, for we will see him as he really is.   1 JOHN 3:2

The Lord isn't really being slow about his promise, as some people think. No, he is being patient for your sake. He does not want anyone to be destroyed, but wants everyone to repent.   2 PETER 3:9

The LORD our God has secrets known to no one. We are not accountable for them, but we and our children are accountable forever for all that he has revealed to us, so that we may obey all the terms of these instructions.   DEUTERONOMY 29:29

*I*f God's nature and knowledge were not beyond human understanding, God would cease to be God. While human beings long to know and understand God and his ways, we must never claim to fully understand him. If we did, we would make ourselves equal to him, at least in our own minds. God's mysteries are opportunities for faith. If you knew everything there was to know about God or his plans for your life, there would be no need for faith. God has given you everything you need to know in order to believe in him and obey him. As you contemplate the mysteries of God, don't forget everything that God has already revealed about himself to you. You are not responsible for what you don't know about God, only for what you do know—and you know that following him is a lifelong adventure of discovery.

DIVINE PROMISE

TRULY, O GOD OF ISRAEL, OUR SAVIOR, YOU WORK IN MYSTERIOUS WAYS.   *Isaiah 45:15*

Nature

MY QUESTION *for* GOD

What does our environment reveal about God?

A MOMENT *with* GOD

God blessed them and said, "Be fruitful and multiply. Fill the earth and govern it. Reign over the fish in the sea, the birds in the sky, and all the animals that scurry along the ground."   GENESIS 1:28

The Lord God placed the man in the Garden of Eden
to tend and watch over it.   Genesis 2:15

When you are attacking a town and the war drags on,
you must not cut down the trees. . . . Are the trees
your enemies, that you should attack them?

Deuteronomy 20:19

The land must have a year of complete rest.

Leviticus 25:5

Let the fields and their crops burst out with joy! Let
the trees of the forest rustle with praise before the
Lord, for he is coming!   Psalm 96:12-13

*T*he Bible teaches us that God cares very much about
all of his creation. When the Israelites went to war, God
was concerned about the needless destruction of the
environment and gave them instructions to protect it.
God's instructions to let the farmland rest every seventh
year allowed for the conservation of good, productive
land. Human beings were created to share responsibility
for the earth by being good stewards of the environment.
The first assignment God gave to Adam was to tend and
care for the Garden of Eden, and he expects you to care
for your little corner of the earth as well. God created
nature to proclaim his glory. You should do whatever
you can to preserve this testimony for God.

Obedience

MY QUESTION *for* GOD

Why is obedience such a big deal to God?

A MOMENT *with* GOD

You must be careful to obey all the commands of the
LORD your God, following his instructions in every
detail.   DEUTERONOMY 5:32

Moses said, "This is what the LORD has commanded
you to do so that the glory of the LORD may appear
to you."   LEVITICUS 9:6

Oh, the joys of those who do not follow the advice
of the wicked, or stand around with sinners, or join
in with mockers. But they delight in the law of the
LORD, meditating on it day and night.   PSALM 1:1-2

God knows you can't obey him completely, so he is
more interested in how much you *want* to obey him.

To want to obey him more, you must grasp a true understanding of obedience and how it builds or destroys relationships. From the teen who arrives home at ten because of his curfew to the student who completes a difficult homework assignment, we all live in a web of relationships that depend upon obedience to authority. Like a loving parent or a responsible teacher, God sets standards of behavior for your own good and to protect you from evil and harm. Some people defy authority, but obedience actually frees us to enjoy life as God intended because it keeps us from becoming entangled in harmful situations. Even though God's commandments are sometimes difficult to obey or don't always make sense from our human perspective, obedience to him will always bring blessing, joy, and peace. When you look at obedience this way, then you will obey God out of love and gratitude for all he's trying to do for you rather than out of fear of being punished. The more you obey out of love, the more you will want to obey, and the more obedience will become a lifestyle rather than a chore. Since God is the creator of life, he knows how life is supposed to work. Obedience to his ways demonstrates your trust that God's way is best and that it will work for you.

DIVINE PROMISE

IF YOU LOOK CAREFULLY INTO THE PERFECT LAW THAT SETS YOU FREE, AND IF YOU DO WHAT IT SAYS AND DON'T FORGET WHAT YOU HEARD, THEN GOD WILL BLESS YOU FOR DOING IT. *James 1:25*

Opportunities

MY QUESTION *for* GOD

How can I make the most of the opportunities that come my way?

A MOMENT *with* GOD

As for Philip, an angel of the Lord said to him, "Go south down the desert road that runs from Jerusalem to Gaza." So he started out, and he met the treasurer of Ethiopia, a eunuch of great authority under the Kandake, the queen of Ethiopia. The eunuch had gone to Jerusalem to worship, and he was now returning. . . . And he urged Philip to come up into the carriage and sit with him.   ACTS 8:26-28, 31

Make the most of every opportunity in these evil days.

EPHESIANS 5:16

Live wisely among those who are not believers, and make the most of every opportunity.   COLOSSIANS 4:5

God had an opportunity waiting for Philip on that desert road. Philip may have felt disappointed at being called away from a thriving ministry, but as a result of following God's leading, a powerful official from a kingdom on another continent believed in God and returned home with the Good News of Jesus. The next time you find yourself in a situation that is not of your choosing, pay careful attention to the leading of God's

Spirit. You may be exactly where God wants you—
on the verge of a divine opportunity!

DIVINE PROMISE

I KNOW ALL THE THINGS YOU DO, AND I HAVE
OPENED A DOOR FOR YOU THAT NO ONE
CAN CLOSE.   *Revelation 3:8*

Overwhelmed

MY QUESTION *for* GOD

*I feel so overwhelmed. How can I overcome the obstacles
I'm facing?*

A MOMENT *with* GOD

So on October 2 the wall was finished—just fifty-
two days after we had begun. When our enemies and
the surrounding nations heard about it, they were
frightened and humiliated. They realized this work
had been done with the help of our God.

NEHEMIAH 6:15-16

Each time he said, "My grace is all you need. My
power works best in weakness." So now I am glad
to boast about my weaknesses, so that the power
of Christ can work through me. That's why I take
pleasure in my weaknesses, and in the insults,
hardships, persecutions, and troubles that I suffer
for Christ. For when I am weak, then I am strong.

2 CORINTHIANS 12:9-10

*J*ust as the Israelites faced the urgent task of rebuilding the wall around their city in a very short period of time, you may also be facing some task or obstacle that seems impossible. You can meet overwhelming challenges of "building the wall" through courageous obedience to what God calls you to do, taking one day at a time. You may think you can't accomplish the bigger work God has planned for you, so try focusing on the little tasks for today. Simply put one brick on top of the other, then trust God to do what you can't do. You do your part, and he'll do the rest—that's all he asks. This is how the big tasks get done. When you begin to see the obstacles in your life as opportunities for God to show his power, they will not seem so overwhelming. The very hardships and weaknesses that frighten you are actually the things that will strengthen your faith. When looking at the obstacles in your path, remember that there is always a little something you can do—lay a brick, make a phone call, write a note, study. In taking small steps of obedience each day, you will build a great work for God one brick at a time.

DIVINE PROMISE

BECAUSE THE SOVEREIGN LORD HELPS ME, I WILL NOT BE DISGRACED. THEREFORE, I HAVE SET MY FACE LIKE A STONE, DETERMINED TO DO HIS WILL. AND I KNOW THAT I WILL NOT BE PUT TO SHAME. *Isaiah 50:7*

Pain

MY QUESTION *for* GOD

Can anything good come out of experiencing pain?

A MOMENT *with* GOD

"Don't tear your clothing in your grief, but tear your hearts instead." Return to the LORD your God, for he is merciful and compassionate.　　　　JOEL 2:13

The sacrifice you desire is a broken spirit. You will not reject a broken and repentant heart, O God.

PSALM 51:17

God is our merciful Father and the source of all comfort. He comforts us in all our troubles so that we can comfort others. When they are troubled, we will be able to give them the same comfort God has given us.　　　　2 CORINTHIANS 1:3-4

You can learn much about God through the pain you experience. Pain can test and prove your commitment to God. Will you move toward him or away from him when you are hurting? Pain can reveal God's power as you see him respond to your cry for help. Pain can be redemptive. Your broken heart can lead you back to God, who heals your soul. Pain equips you to comfort others in their pain because you know what they are going through. It is easier to deal with pain when someone helps you through it. God feels your pain. He knows what you are going through and is in the best position to help you. As God helps you through your pain, he teaches you to help others through their pain. Allow these times to strengthen your faith, your character, and your compassion for others.

DIVINE PROMISE

YET WHAT WE SUFFER NOW IS NOTHING COMPARED TO THE GLORY HE WILL REVEAL TO US LATER. *Romans 8:18*

Panic

MY QUESTION *for* GOD

How do I keep from panicking when things seem to be crashing in around me?

A MOMENT *with* GOD

As Pharaoh approached, the people of Israel looked up and panicked when they saw the Egyptians overtaking them. They cried out to the LORD, and they said to Moses, "Why did you bring us out here to die in the wilderness?" EXODUS 14:10-11

Troubles surround me—too many to count! My sins pile up so high I can't see my way out. They outnumber the hairs on my head. I have lost all courage. PSALM 40:12

Fear and trembling overwhelm me, and I can't
stop shaking.   PSALM 55:5

Call on me when you are in trouble, and I will rescue
you, and you will give me glory.   PSALM 50:15

*P*anic is physically and emotionally paralyzing—worry
and fear meet in instant crisis. You've had no time to
prepare for it, and you're too frozen with fear to deal
with it. If you haven't experienced panic before or if you
haven't prepared for it, you won't be able to deal well
with it when it hits. You prepare for panic by learning
to let go of what you can't control. God's job is to rescue you; your job is to trust God and then give him the
credit. What a comfort! Trouble is an opportunity to
experience God's peace, not panic. Often, though, it
is easy to get things backwards. You only make matters
worse when you try to rescue yourself. A key to success
in life—especially when facing challenges—is to let go
of what you can't control and remember that God cares
for you and is always in control. When your security
is anchored in the knowledge that God is in control of
your soul and your circumstances, you will experience
overwhelming peace rather than panic.

DIVINE PROMISE

WHEN THE EARTH QUAKES AND ITS PEOPLE
LIVE IN TURMOIL, I AM THE ONE WHO KEEPS
ITS FOUNDATIONS FIRM. *Psalm 75:3*

Passion

Why can't I always be on fire for God?

King Solomon loved many foreign women. . . . He married women from Moab, Ammon, Edom, Sidon, and from among the Hittites. The LORD had clearly instructed the people, . . . "You must not marry them, because they will turn your hearts to their gods." Yet Solomon insisted on loving them anyway. . . . And in fact, they did turn his heart away from the LORD.   1 KINGS 11:1-3

When sin gets a foothold in your life, it always leads you away from God, which in turn makes you feel apathetic toward him. Satan always tries his best to keep you from getting excited about following God.

The woman was convinced. She saw that the tree was beautiful and its fruit looked delicious, and she wanted the wisdom it would give her. So she took some of the fruit and ate it. Then she gave some to her husband, who was with her, and he ate it, too.

                                                GENESIS 3:6

Temptation can take your focus off God and make something else seem more exciting. It's not that you really want to move away from God, but something else suddenly gets your attention! If what you're excited about is not what God wants you to do, your passion for God will quickly die.

They went to the olive grove called Gethsemane, and Jesus said, . . . "Stay here and keep watch with me." He went on a little farther and fell to the ground. He prayed that, if it were possible, the awful hour awaiting him might pass him by. "Abba, Father," he cried out, "everything is possible for you. Please take this cup of suffering away from me. Yet I want your will to be done, not mine." Then he returned and found the disciples asleep. He said to Peter, "Simon, are you asleep? Couldn't you watch with me even one hour? Keep watch and pray, so that you will not give in to temptation. For the spirit is willing, but the body is weak."   MARK 14:32-38

*S*ometimes you're just too tired or you don't see the significance of what is going on around you. You must be passionate about looking for God in every circumstance.

You must continue to believe this truth and stand firmly in it. Don't drift away from the assurance you received when you heard the Good News. The Good News has been preached all over the world, and I, Paul, have been appointed as God's servant to proclaim it.   COLOSSIANS 1:23

We must listen very carefully to the truth we have heard, or we may drift away from it.   HEBREWS 2:1

I have this complaint against you. You don't love me
or each other as you did at first!   REVELATION 2:4

𝓛ike all relationships, your relationship with God
takes effort and energy. God is always fully committed
to you. For your relationship with God to be exciting, you must be fully committed to him. Be diligent
in your efforts to get to know him better. Here are
four strategies for doing that: Consistently study God's
Word, communicate with God in prayer, cultivate a
thankful heart, and engage in acts of service to others.
These will help fight off feelings of apathy toward God
and renew your passion for the purpose he has for your
life. You will again be excited about the blessings he has
given you and has promised you in the future.

DIVINE PROMISE

I WILL GIVE THEM SINGLENESS OF HEART AND
PUT A NEW SPIRIT WITHIN THEM. I WILL TAKE
AWAY THEIR STONY, STUBBORN HEART AND
GIVE THEM A TENDER, RESPONSIVE HEART.
Ezekiel 11:19

𝓟ast

MY QUESTION *for* GOD

*I've done some bad things in the past. Can I really lead a
godly life today?*

A MOMENT *with* GOD

When I refused to confess my sin, my body wasted
away, and I groaned all day long. Day and night your
hand of discipline was heavy on me. My strength
evaporated like water in the summer heat. Finally,
I confessed all my sins to you and stopped trying to
hide my guilt. I said to myself, "I will confess my
rebellion to the LORD." And you forgave me! All my
guilt is gone.   PSALM 32:3-5

I will delight in your decrees and not forget your
word. . . . I will never forget your commandments,
for by them you give me life.   PSALM 119:16, 93

Though your sins are like scarlet, I will make them
as white as snow. Though they are red like crimson,
I will make them as white as wool.   ISAIAH 1:18

The past is like a photo album containing snapshots
of every moment of your life. These snapshots show
not just your happy moments and celebrations, but also
your failures, tragedies, and acts of deepest shame.
Most of us would like to lock away some parts of our
past or tear out the snapshots that expose the moments
we'd like to forget. The apostle Paul, one of the greatest heroes in the Bible, had a past he wished he could
forget. His album was full of snapshots recording his
days of persecuting and killing Christians. Paul could
have been burdened with immense regret, but he understood that his past had been redeemed through
God's healing and forgiveness. How you view your past

affects how you live in the present and in the future. Some of us have a past containing a strong spiritual heritage from loving parents and mentors. Don't take that for granted; use it to help and minister to others. Some of us have a past filled with regret over actions that were wrong or hurtful. Some of us have a tragic past marred by abuse, neglect, violence, or the shameful acts of other people. No matter what you've done or what's been done to you, God is ready to forgive you, heal you, cleanse you of sin and guilt, and give you a new start—fully forgiven. God wants to throw away all the bad snapshots and give you a new present and future—and he can if you'll let him. God can remove your regret, guilt, and shame, and you can be free to live in peace with purpose and joy.

DIVINE PROMISE

I WILL FORGIVE THEIR WICKEDNESS, AND I WILL NEVER AGAIN REMEMBER THEIR SINS.
Hebrews 8:12

Patience

MY QUESTION *for* GOD

How can I learn to be more patient?

A Moment *with* God

May God, who gives this patience and encouragement, help you live in complete harmony with each
other, as is fitting for followers of Christ Jesus.

ROMANS 15:5

Be patient with each other, making allowance for
each other's faults because of your love.   EPHESIANS 4:2

We also pray that you will be strengthened with all
his glorious power so you will have all the endurance
and patience you need.   COLOSSIANS 1:11

*P*atience and perspective go hand in hand. When you
are always focused on your own agenda and priorities,
you will be impatient much of the time because life
rarely goes exactly the way you want it to. But if you
have a broader perspective and see life as a winding
journey instead of a straight line between two points,
you will realize that what you do along the way is often
more important than getting there. This allows you to
be patient when things don't seem to be going the right
way. It also helps you discover ways to serve others on
the detours of daily life.

Divine Promise

PATIENT ENDURANCE IS WHAT YOU NEED
NOW, SO THAT YOU WILL CONTINUE TO DO
GOD'S WILL. THEN YOU WILL RECEIVE ALL THAT
HE HAS PROMISED.   *Hebrews 10:36*

Peace

MY QUESTION *for* GOD

Often there is more confusion and turmoil in my heart than peace. How can I have more peace?

A MOMENT *with* GOD

In peace I will lie down and sleep, for you alone,
O LORD, will keep me safe.   PSALM 4:8

The LORD gives his people strength. The LORD
blesses them with peace.   PSALM 29:11

You are my hiding place; you protect me from
trouble. You surround me with songs of victory.

PSALM 32:7

*Y*ou can have peace despite your circumstances when
you fully trust that God is always watching over your
soul. This sounds so simple, but it actually takes a courageous step of faith. The peace of God will not prevent
you from encountering difficulties, but it will give you
the final victory over them. God promises to give you
eternal life in heaven if you accept his free gift of salvation, and he promises that Satan cannot take these gifts
away. When you have total confidence in these two
things, then no matter what happens, you will experience the inner peace that comes from knowing God.

DIVINE PROMISE

I AM LEAVING YOU WITH A GIFT—PEACE OF
MIND AND HEART. AND THE PEACE I GIVE IS A
GIFT THE WORLD CANNOT GIVE. SO DON'T BE
TROUBLED OR AFRAID.   *John 14:27*

Perfection

MY QUESTION *for* GOD

How could perfectionism limit my ability to experience God?

A MOMENT *with* GOD

Farmers who wait for perfect weather never plant.
If they watch every cloud, they never harvest.

ECCLESIASTES 11:4

Even perfection has its limits, but your commands
have no limit.   PSALM 119:96

*P*erfectionism can act as a barrier to action. It is not
necessary to always wait for the perfect opportunity;
just obediently follow God and his commands at every opportunity. In fact, God loves working through
imperfect people and circumstances. Sometimes the
biggest disasters are the best opportunities for experiencing the unlimited power of God.

DIVINE PROMISE

JESUS LOOKED AT THEM INTENTLY AND SAID,
"HUMANLY SPEAKING, IT IS IMPOSSIBLE. BUT
WITH GOD EVERYTHING IS POSSIBLE."

Matthew 19:26

Persecution

MY QUESTION *for* GOD

*Why is it so important to endure persecution rather than give
in to it?*

A MOMENT *with* GOD

That's why I take pleasure in my weaknesses, and
in the insults, hardships, persecutions, and troubles
that I suffer for Christ. For when I am weak, then I
am strong.   2 CORINTHIANS 12:10

We can rejoice, too, when we run into problems
and trials, for we know that they help us develop
endurance. And endurance develops strength
of character.   ROMANS 5:3-4

God promises special blessings to those who hang
on to their faith in him, no matter what happens. For
your faith to become strong and genuine, you will
likely need to endure testing. Sometimes the hardest
test is being scorned, mocked, or ignored by others
because of your faith in God. It is during these hard

times that your character is revealed and forced to grow. How you handle persecution shows who you really are on the inside, and it reveals your level of commitment to God. By enduring persecution, you show that your faith and trust in God is real. The Bible tells us about many people who never stopped trusting God even though they were mocked, persecuted, and even killed for their faith. You may never face martyrdom for being a Christian, but is your faith strong enough to endure even a little derision or scorn? Those who live boldly for God, despite opposition, make a great impact for eternity.

DIVINE PROMISE

THE MORE WE SUFFER FOR CHRIST, THE MORE GOD WILL SHOWER US WITH HIS COMFORT THROUGH CHRIST.   *2 Corinthians 1:5*

Perspective

MY QUESTIONS *for* GOD

How do I understand the seemingly random circumstances of my life? Is God really in charge, or do things just happen by chance?

A MOMENT *with* GOD

I am Joseph, your brother, whom you sold into slavery in Egypt. But don't be upset, and don't be angry with yourselves for selling me to this place.

It was God who sent me here ahead of you to preserve
your lives. . . . So it was God who sent me here,
not you!   GENESIS 45:4-5, 8

The LORD will work out his plans for my life.

PSALM 138:8

𝔉rom our human perspective, the world and even our
lives often seem to be random and unpredictable, but
God is ultimately in control. In Joseph's life, God used
even the unjust treatment that Joseph received from
his own brothers to fulfill his plan. The sinful ways of
people do not ruin the sovereign plans of God. Life is
like a tapestry. Now you can see only some sections
of the back, which is full of knots and loose ends. But
someday you will see the front of the tapestry in its
beautiful entirety—the picture of world history as well
as your personal history from God's perspective. If you
can accept unexpected and even unwelcome circumstances in this way, you'll be able to embrace both the
good and the bad because you trust that God is weaving
a beautiful picture with your life.

DIVINE PROMISE
YOU SEE ME WHEN I TRAVEL AND WHEN I REST
AT HOME. YOU KNOW EVERYTHING I DO.
Psalm 139:3

Perspective

MY QUESTION *for* GOD

How can I learn to see others from God's perspective?

A MOMENT *with* GOD

There will be weeping and gnashing of teeth, for you will see Abraham, Isaac, Jacob, and all the prophets in the Kingdom of God, but you will be thrown out. And people will come from all over the world—from east and west, north and south—to take their places in the Kingdom of God. And note this: Some who seem least important now will be the greatest then, and some who are the greatest now will be least important then.

LUKE 13:28-30

*J*esus says that a big surprise awaits those who arrive in heaven. Lots of people you may not have expected to see will be there, and lots of people you were certain would be there will be absent. And many people may indeed be surprised to see you there! In these verses, Jesus pictures those with impeccable spiritual pedigrees not making the cut, while a whole crowd of spiritual nobodies are in. Part of Jesus' message here is to challenge you to see people from God's perspective. A person's spiritual status comes not from culturally defined goodness or even from doing lots of good things for others but from humbly receiving salvation through faith in Jesus Christ. People are marked as God's people not by being religious but by having a relationship with Jesus. Think of how many divine moments and breakthroughs are missed when we presume to know someone's eternal destiny. Learn to see others from God's perspective, and you'll never miss out on a divine moment!

DIVINE PROMISE

THOSE THE FATHER HAS GIVEN ME WILL COME TO ME, AND I WILL NEVER REJECT THEM.
John 6:37

Plans

MY QUESTION *for* GOD

How can I make plans that are in line with God's will?

A MOMENT *with* GOD

I have a plan for the whole earth, a hand of judgment upon all the nations. The LORD of Heaven's Armies has spoken—who can change his plans? When his hand is raised, who can stop him?   ISAIAH 14:26-27

The LORD will work out his plans for my life.

PSALM 138:8

"I know the plans I have for you," says the LORD. "They are plans for good and not for disaster, to give you a future and a hope."

JEREMIAH 29:11

Some people think that making plans shows a lack of faith in God's plans, but it is good planning that helps you put your faith in God into action. When making plans, you should always be mindful of God's revealed plans laid out in the Bible. God has a general plan for everyone, but he also has a specific plan for you. He uniquely created you to fulfill that plan, so you need to find out what it is. The frustrating thing is that he doesn't always make his plan for you crystal clear. He does that for a reason—he wants you to walk step-by-step with him in faith, trusting him to show you just enough to help you take the next step but not so much that you feel you don't need his guidance anymore. The most important step you can take each day to discover God's plan for you is to read his Word and obey it. As you follow through on your plans to obey God, you will be able to recognize when God is leading you in another direction and you will be equipped to make new plans and follow through on them. Sometimes it's not until you've made your plans and acted on them that you can see God's divine guidance in your life.

DIVINE PROMISE

YOU CAN MAKE MANY PLANS, BUT THE LORD'S PURPOSE WILL PREVAIL. *Proverbs 19:21*

Pleasure

MY QUESTION for GOD

What is the best perspective on enjoying pleasure in this life?

A MOMENT with GOD

I said to myself, "Come on, let's try pleasure. Let's look for the 'good things' in life." But I found that this, too, was meaningless. So I said, "Laughter is silly. What good does it do to seek pleasure?" After much thought, I decided to cheer myself with wine. And while still seeking wisdom, I clutched at foolishness. In this way, I tried to experience the only happiness most people find during their brief life in this world. . . . But as I looked at everything I had worked so hard to accomplish, it was all so meaningless—like chasing the wind. There was nothing really worthwhile anywhere.

ECCLESIASTES 2:1-3, 11

You will show me the way of life, granting me the joy of your presence and the pleasures of living with you forever.   PSALM 16:11

In his search for fulfillment, Solomon devoted his considerable resources to the pursuit of pleasure. The Bible tells us that he eventually collected seven hundred wives and one thousand concubines. Yet he discovered that the pursuit of pleasure is like running on a treadmill that never stops. The need for pleasure can become like an addiction—relentless and impossible to fully satisfy. In fact, chasing after pleasure can dull you to the effects of sin. Don't let today's fun seal tomorrow's spiritual fate. Although the pleasures of this life are not necessarily evil, neither do they bring ultimate meaning to your life. God created your need for pleasure to be met through a relationship with him. Pleasure without God is empty; you always need more in order to feel good. Taking pleasure in what God is doing in your life is a source of satisfaction. The greatest pleasures come from pleasing God and experiencing the peace and joy of a faithful life.

DIVINE PROMISE

OH, THE JOYS OF THOSE WHO DO NOT FOLLOW THE ADVICE OF THE WICKED.... BUT THEY DELIGHT IN THE LAW OF THE LORD. *Psalm 1:1-2*

Potential

MY QUESTION *for* GOD

How can I achieve my God-given potential?

A MOMENT *with* GOD

The LORD says, "O Israel, when I first found you, it was like finding fresh grapes in the desert. When I saw your ancestors, it was like seeing the first ripe figs of the season. But then they deserted me for Baal-peor, giving themselves to that shameful idol. Soon they became vile, as vile as the god they worshiped."

HOSEA 9:10

Because of the privilege and authority God has given
me, I give each of you this warning: Don't think
you are better than you really are. Be honest in your
evaluation of yourselves, measuring yourselves by the
faith God has given us.   ROMANS 12:3

We are God's masterpiece. He has created us anew in
Christ Jesus, so we can do the good things he planned
for us long ago.   EPHESIANS 2:10

*W*asted potential is a tragic thing. You are created in
the image of a loving and holy God, which means you
have the potential to reflect all of his marvelous characteristics. If you decide not to follow God, you are de-
ciding not to live up to the potential for which you were
created. But if you have faith in God, you can begin to
develop your spiritual potential by giving him control
of your life. The Holy Spirit then comes to live in your
heart and helps you reach the spiritual potential for
which you were created—to reflect God's holiness and
to use your spiritual gifts in helping others. Your full
potential is found in what God can do through you, not
what you can do by yourself. Take an honest appraisal
of yourself; you don't want to be proud because of the
gifts and abilities God has given you, yet you don't want
to be so self-effacing that you fail to use your gifts and
abilities for God's glory.

DIVINE PROMISE

I AM CERTAIN THAT GOD, WHO BEGAN THE
GOOD WORK WITHIN YOU, WILL CONTINUE
HIS WORK UNTIL IT IS FINALLY FINISHED ON
THE DAY WHEN CHRIST JESUS RETURNS.

Philippians 1:6

Power of God

MY QUESTION *for* GOD

How can I experience God's power working through me?

A MOMENT *with* GOD

Each time he said, "My grace is all you need. My
power works best in weakness." So now I am glad
to boast about my weaknesses, so that the power of
Christ can work through me.   2 CORINTHIANS 12:9

God wanted them to know that the riches and glory
of Christ are for you Gentiles, too. And this is the
secret: Christ lives in you. This gives you assurance
of sharing his glory. . . . I work and struggle so hard,
depending on Christ's mighty power that works
within me.   COLOSSIANS 1:27-29

Be strong in the Lord and in his mighty power. Put
on all of God's armor so that you will be able to stand
firm against all strategies of the devil. For we are not
fighting against flesh-and-blood enemies, but against
evil rulers and authorities of the unseen world,

against mighty powers in this dark world, and against
evil spirits in the heavenly places.   EPHESIANS 6:10-12

*I*t seems logical that only a strong person would have
the capacity to experience the power of God. But God's
power is not dependent on human strength. In fact,
God's power is best seen through weaknesses. When
you are weak, it is only by God's strength that you
can accomplish what you could not do on your own.
God's power comes from his presence within you. You
do not merely imitate him—by trying through your
own efforts to do right and seek his will—you have
the living God—his Holy Spirit and his power—working through you. As God's power works in you, you
grow spiritually. Spiritual growth is likely to stir up
spiritual opposition. Spiritual battles require spiritual
power. God's armor provides the power you need to
stand against the schemes of the world and the devil.
When problems come up, don't look at the size of the
problem but at the size of your God. There are great
things to be done, and you have a great God who will
do them through you.

DIVINE PROMISE

WITH GOD'S HELP WE WILL DO
MIGHTY THINGS.   *Psalm 60:12*

Prayer

My Question *for* God

Does God always answer prayer?

A Moment *with* God

I love the LORD because he hears my voice and my
prayer for mercy.   PSALM 116:1

Three different times I begged the Lord to take it
away. Each time he said, " . . . My power works best
in weakness."   2 CORINTHIANS 12:8-9

If you remain in me and my words remain in you,
you may ask for anything you want, and it will
be granted!   JOHN 15:7

❧❧❧

God listens carefully to every prayer and answers each
one. His answer may be yes, no, or wait, just as loving
parents might give each of these three responses to the
requests of their child. Answering yes to every request
would spoil you and endanger your well-being. Answering no to every request would be vindictive, stingy, and
hard on your spirit. Answering wait to every request
would frustrate you. God always answers your prayers
according to what he knows is best for you. Knowing
that God always listens and answers should inspire you
to pray continually, even if his answer is not always the
one you wanted. When you don't get the answer you
want, don't interpret it to mean that God hasn't heard
you; rather, look for how it might be pointing you in a

different direction. You will grow in spiritual maturity as you seek to understand why God's answers to your prayers are in your best interest.

DIVINE PROMISE

THE EYES OF THE LORD WATCH OVER THOSE WHO DO RIGHT, AND HIS EARS ARE OPEN TO THEIR PRAYERS.   *1 Peter 3:12*

Prayer

MY QUESTION *for* GOD

How do I talk to God?

A MOMENT *with* GOD

I confess my sins; I am deeply sorry for what I have done.   PSALM 38:18

I will praise you, LORD, with all my heart. . . . I will sing praises to your name, O Most High.   PSALM 9:1-2

Keep on asking, and you will receive what you ask for. Keep on seeking, and you will find. Keep on knocking, and the door will be opened to you. For everyone who asks, receives. Everyone who seeks, finds. And to everyone who knocks, the door will be opened. You parents—if your children ask for a loaf of bread, do you give them a stone instead? Or if they ask for a fish, do you give them a snake? Of course not! So if you sinful people know how to give good gifts to your children, how much more will your heavenly Father give good gifts to those who ask him.

MATTHEW 7:7-11

*P*rayer is talking to God and building a relationship with him. When you talk to God, you can praise and thank him, make requests, confess sins, express pain and frustration, and simply share what is happening in your life. Good conversation also includes listening, so allow time for God to speak to you. When you listen to God, he can make his wisdom and resources available to you. Prayer can also soften your heart and help you avoid the debilitating effects of anger, resentment, and bitterness. There's so much more to prayer than just getting an answer to a question or a solution for a problem. God often does more in your heart through your act of prayer than he does through the actual answer to your prayer. As you persist in talking and listening to God, he promises that you will gain greater understanding of yourself and your situation as well as his nature and his direction for your life.

DIVINE PROMISE

DON'T WORRY ABOUT ANYTHING; INSTEAD, PRAY ABOUT EVERYTHING. TELL GOD WHAT YOU NEED, AND THANK HIM FOR ALL HE HAS DONE. THEN YOU WILL EXPERIENCE GOD'S PEACE, WHICH EXCEEDS ANYTHING WE CAN UNDERSTAND. HIS PEACE WILL GUARD

YOUR HEARTS AND MINDS AS YOU LIVE IN
CHRIST JESUS.   *Philippians 4:6-7*

Pressure

MY QUESTION *for* GOD

*My friends put a lot of pressure on me to do what I know is
wrong. How can I deal with this kind of pressure?*

A MOMENT *with* GOD

[Ahab] turned to Jehoshaphat and asked, "Will
you join me in battle to recover Ramoth-gilead?"
Jehoshaphat replied to the king of Israel, "Why, of
course! You and I are as one. My troops are your
troops, and my horses are your horses. . . . But first
let's find out what the LORD says." . . . The king of
Israel replied to Jehoshaphat, "There is one more man
who could consult the LORD for us, but I hate him."

                                                1 KINGS 22:4-5, 8

*A*hab was a king who wanted nothing to do with
God. Jehoshaphat was a king who sincerely tried to
follow God. Jehoshaphat made a huge mistake when he
called evil King Ahab his brother and joined with him
in war, going against the advice of God's prophet. As a
result, the battle was a disaster. Whenever you are facing the pressure to do anything that you know would
displease God, your best course of action may be to remove yourself from the situation. Sometimes you must

do more than say no—you must walk away. Otherwise you, too, may be headed for trouble. That hesitation or heavy feeling in your heart before you do something may be God's way of getting your attention before the pressure becomes too great for you to handle. When you feel the familiar push of pressure, thank God for the warning, and do what you must to get away!

DIVINE PROMISE

DON'T TEAM UP WITH THOSE WHO ARE UNBELIEVERS. HOW CAN RIGHTEOUSNESS BE A PARTNER WITH WICKEDNESS?   *2 Corinthians 6:14*

Priorities

MY QUESTION *for* GOD

How can I manage all of my life's demands if I make God my first priority?

A MOMENT *with* GOD

Saul built an altar to the LORD; it was the first of the altars he built to the LORD.   1 SAMUEL 14:35

Then Saul said, "Let's chase the Philistines all night and plunder them until sunrise. Let's destroy every last one of them." His men replied, "We'll do whatever you think is best." But the priest said, "Let's ask God first."   1 SAMUEL 14:36

*I*magine that you're in the middle of a very personal and significant conversation with a friend when your cell phone rings. What do you do? Most of us would answer the phone, or at least check the caller ID. Why? Because interruptions tend to become top priorities. Our lives seem to skip from one urgent interruption to another. And all the while, we keep missing what is really important. What are the things that matter most in life, that are true priorities? How can we distinguish true priorities from lesser ones, like the ringing phone? The answer is this: Don't confuse what's urgent with what's important. Saul had trouble making God his first priority. He failed to build an altar to God until months or possibly years after he was anointed king. Then in the urgency of the moment he tried to rush a decision about attacking his enemies without consulting God. In both cases, something that seemed urgent took Saul away from what he really needed to be doing—worshiping and consulting God. The key to managing the demands of life is to set your priorities early. Putting God first in your life helps put all of your other priorities in order. Don't let everyone else decide what your day should look like—that should be between you and God. If you make God your first priority, he will give you the proper perspective on the rest of the activities in your day. Ask God to show you what is worth being concerned about. There is no greater priority than loving and obeying God. Nothing else affects your eternal future so significantly.

DIVINE PROMISE

SEEK THE KINGDOM OF GOD ABOVE ALL ELSE,
AND LIVE RIGHTEOUSLY, AND HE WILL GIVE
YOU EVERYTHING YOU NEED.   *Matthew 6:33*

Promises of God

MY QUESTION *for* GOD

*What is the comfort in knowing that God will keep
his promises?*

A MOMENT *with* GOD

God has given both his promise and his oath. These
two things are unchangeable because it is impossible
for God to lie.   HEBREWS 6:18

No, I will not break my covenant; I will not take back
a single word I said. . . . I cannot lie.   PSALM 89:34-35

This truth gives them confidence that they have
eternal life, which God—who does not lie—
promised them before the world began.   TITUS 1:2

Have you ever wondered if there is anything God
cannot do? Actually, there is something: God cannot
lie. God didn't just create truth; he *is* truth. Therefore, God's promises are completely dependable and
trustworthy because God cannot lie—there is no un-
truth or sin in him. So when God makes a promise, it
will happen. God has made hundreds of promises in

his Word, the Bible. Many of these promises are given to everyone who has faith in him, including you. If you want to grow in your faith, if you want to trust God more, if you want to eliminate some of your doubts, if you need more confidence that obeying God is the right thing to do—then you must diligently study the Bible just as you would study for an important test. Then you will discover God's promises to you. This kind of study has more than just earthly rewards—it has eternal rewards. Each promise you discover gives you a divine moment in which you see how much God loves you and wants to have a relationship with you, and what you must do to experience the full benefits of his promises. Start your Bible study today—don't delay. Your life can be an adventure and take on a whole new meaning when you discover everything God has promised you.

DIVINE PROMISE

LET US HOLD TIGHTLY WITHOUT WAVERING
TO THE HOPE WE AFFIRM, FOR GOD CAN BE
TRUSTED TO KEEP HIS PROMISE.   *Hebrews 10:23*

Promises of God

MY QUESTION *for* GOD

Which promises of God impact my life today?

A Moment *with* God

The Lord your God will personally go ahead of you.
He will neither fail you nor abandon you.

Deuteronomy 31:6

Now I will send the Holy Spirit, just as my Father
promised.   Luke 24:49

If we confess our sins to him, he is faithful and just
to forgive us our sins and to cleanse us from all
wickedness.   1 John 1:9

Since we have been made right in God's sight by faith,
we have peace with God because of what Jesus Christ
our Lord has done for us.   Romans 5:1

Jesus said, "Come to me, all of you who are weary
and carry heavy burdens, and I will give you rest. . . .
You will find rest for your souls."   Matthew 11:28-29

Sometimes you may feel like God is far away or even
irrelevant to your daily life. But think about the promises in the above verses. God has promised to be with
you always in the form of the Holy Spirit. He has promised to forgive your sins, to give you peace of heart
and mind, to carry your burdens, and to give you rest.
How much more meaningful and relevant to your life
could his promises be? And these are just a fraction of
the promises God has given you. With God always by
your side, you don't need to be afraid. With God forgiving your sins, you don't need to feel guilty anymore.
This gives you the motivation to overcome temptations

instead of succumbing to them. God carries your burdens so you can be free from worry and anxiety. Talk about peace of mind and heart! Which of these promises do you need to hold on to today? Thank God that he has promised all of these things and that he is faithful in keeping his promises.

DIVINE PROMISE

O LORD, GOD OF ISRAEL, THERE IS NO GOD LIKE YOU IN ALL OF HEAVEN ABOVE OR ON THE EARTH BELOW. YOU KEEP YOUR COVENANT AND SHOW UNFAILING LOVE TO ALL WHO WALK BEFORE YOU IN WHOLEHEARTED DEVOTION. *1 Kings 8:23*

Purpose

MY QUESTION *for* GOD

Why am I here?

A MOMENT *with* GOD

"I knew you before I formed you in your mother's womb. Before you were born I set you apart." . . . "O Sovereign LORD," I said, "I can't speak for you! I'm too young!" The LORD replied, "Don't say, 'I'm too young,' for you must go wherever I send you and say whatever I tell you." JEREMIAH 1:5-7

I cry out to God Most High, to God who will fulfill his purpose for me. PSALM 57:2

You can make many plans, but the LORD's purpose
will prevail.   PROVERBS 19:21

*G*od created you for a purpose. It only makes sense
that your Creator knows exactly what will satisfy the
longings of your heart. You have the choice either to
follow God and do what he already knows will fulfill
you and make a difference in this world, or to go your
own way. How much better to pursue God's plan for
you! Then you'll be sure that your life will have meaning, and you will accomplish what God created you
to do. Sometimes it takes years to find your purpose,
and sometimes you know it at a young age. Never stop
searching—the searching keeps you close to God.

DIVINE PROMISE

YOU MADE ALL THE DELICATE, INNER PARTS
OF MY BODY AND KNIT ME TOGETHER IN MY
MOTHER'S WOMB. . . . YOU SAW ME BEFORE
I WAS BORN. EVERY DAY OF MY LIFE WAS
RECORDED IN YOUR BOOK. EVERY MOMENT
WAS LAID OUT BEFORE A SINGLE DAY HAD
PASSED. HOW PRECIOUS ARE YOUR THOUGHTS
ABOUT ME, O GOD. THEY CANNOT BE
NUMBERED! *Psalm 139:13, 16-17*

Purpose

MY QUESTION *for* GOD

How do I find God's specific purpose for my life?

A MOMENT *with* GOD

I cry out to God Most High, to God who will fulfill
his purpose for me.   PSALM 57:2

My life is worth nothing to me unless I use it for
finishing the work assigned me by the Lord Jesus.

                                                  ACTS 20:24

You didn't choose me. I chose you. I appointed you to
go and produce lasting fruit, so that the Father will
give you whatever you ask for, using my name.

                                                  JOHN 15:16

I take joy in doing your will, my God, for your
instructions are written on my heart.   PSALM 40:8

I press on to possess that perfection for which Christ
Jesus first possessed me.   PHILIPPIANS 3:12

Do you keep a to-do list of the things you need to
accomplish each day, week, or month? Such lists can
bring a sense of purpose to your life because they help
you stay focused and on target. If you were to reduce
your entire life's goals to a list of only three or four
items, what would they be? The top item on that list
should come close to identifying the purpose of your
life. According to the Bible, your purpose is to be in-

spired with a vision of how God can best use you to accomplish his goals. God has both a general purpose and a specific purpose for you. In a general sense, you have been chosen by God to let the love of Jesus shine through you to make an impact on others. More specifically, God has given you unique spiritual gifts and wants you to use them to make a contribution within your sphere of influence. The more you fulfill your general purpose, the clearer your specific purpose will become. Your ultimate goal in life should not be to reach the destinations you want but to reach the destinations God wants for you. As you passionately pursue the purpose God has assigned you, God promises to give your life greater meaning, lasting significance, and eternal results.

DIVINE PROMISE

LET GOD TRANSFORM YOU INTO A NEW
PERSON BY CHANGING THE WAY YOU THINK.
THEN YOU WILL LEARN TO KNOW GOD'S WILL
FOR YOU, WHICH IS GOOD AND PLEASING
AND PERFECT.   *Romans 12:2*

Questions

MY QUESTION *for* GOD

What are some important questions I should ask myself each day?

A Moment *with* God

The crowds asked, "What should we do?"   LUKE 3:10

Shouldn't people ask God for guidance?   ISAIAH 8:19

Search for the LORD and for his strength; continually
seek him.   PSALM 105:4

Hear me as I pray, O LORD. Be merciful and
answer me!   PSALM 27:7

Are you the Messiah we've been expecting, or should
we keep looking for someone else?   MATTHEW 11:3

Do you have the gift of speaking? Then speak as
though God himself were speaking through you.
Do you have the gift of helping others? Do it with
all the strength and energy that God supplies. Then
everything you do will bring glory to God through
Jesus Christ.   1 PETER 4:11

Even the Son of Man came not to be served but to
serve others and to give his life as a ransom for many.

                                                 MARK 10:45

*P*erhaps nothing reveals what's inside of you more
than the questions you are asking every day. Questions
reveal who you are, what you're thinking about, what
you long to know, and what drives you. Here are some
questions that can shape who you are on the inside if
you ask them every day: Am I changing for better or
for worse? Will my plans for today please God? Will I
be serving others? Asking questions like these will help

you decide how to spend your time and will begin to
change you to be more like Jesus.

DIVINE PROMISE

THIS IS WHAT THE LORD SAYS . . . : ASK ME AND
I WILL TELL YOU REMARKABLE SECRETS YOU
DO NOT KNOW.   *Jeremiah 33:2-3*

Quiet Time

MY QUESTION *for* GOD

How important is it to have quiet time with God?

A MOMENT *with* GOD

Be still, and know that I am God! I will be honored
by every nation. I will be honored throughout
the world.   PSALM 46:10

Finding times to be quiet and meditate will help you
recognize the voice of God when he speaks to you.

Then Jesus said, "Let's go off by ourselves to a quiet
place and rest awhile." He said this because there
were so many people coming and going that Jesus and
his apostles didn't even have time to eat. So they left
by boat for a quiet place.   MARK 6:31-32

$\mathcal{J}$esus knew it was important to spend time with people, but he also knew the importance of rest and reflection. Your life should have a balance between working and resting, spending time with people and having quiet time for restoration.

Only in returning to me and resting in me
will you be saved. In quietness and confidence is
your strength.   ISAIAH 30:15

$\mathcal{I}$t is crucial to renew your relationship with God and be restored by spending time with him. Connecting with God allows you to tap into his strength.

"Go out and stand before me on the mountain," the LORD told him. And as Elijah stood there, the LORD passed by, and a mighty windstorm hit the mountain. It was such a terrible blast that the rocks were torn loose, but the LORD was not in the wind. After the wind there was an earthquake, but the LORD was not in the earthquake. And after the earthquake there was a fire, but the LORD was not in the fire. And after the fire there was the sound of a gentle whisper. When Elijah heard it, he wrapped his face in his cloak and went out and stood at the entrance of the cave. And a voice said, "What are you doing here, Elijah?"

1 KINGS 19:11-13

$\mathcal{S}$ometimes you must be still and quiet to prepare yourself for hearing God speak. Sometimes you must

spend time in his presence without feeling the need
to verbalize your prayers. Meditate on God and listen
for his voice. Be ready to hear him speak to your heart
and mind.

When you pray, go away by yourself, shut the door
behind you, and pray to your Father in private. Then
your Father, who sees everything, will reward you.

MATTHEW 6:6

*Q*uiet times allow you to escape from the busy world
so you can feel free to be open with God.

Guard your heart above all else, for it determines the
course of your life.   PROVERBS 4:23

I wait quietly before God, for my victory comes from
him. . . . Let all that I am wait quietly before God,
for my hope is in him. . . . Pour out your heart to
him, for God is our refuge.   PSALM 62:1, 5, 8

*D*uring quiet times, train yourself so that you will
have the spiritual wisdom, strength, and commitment
to honor God in the face of intense desires and temptations. The best time to prepare for temptation is before
it hits you.

DIVINE CHALLENGE

CLOTHE YOURSELVES INSTEAD WITH THE
BEAUTY THAT COMES FROM WITHIN, THE

UNFADING BEAUTY OF A GENTLE AND QUIET
SPIRIT, WHICH IS SO PRECIOUS TO GOD.
1 Peter 3:3-4

Regrets

My Question *for* God

*There are a lot of things in my past I regret doing. How can
I get over those regrets?*

A Moment *with* God

Meanwhile, Peter was sitting outside in the
courtyard. A servant girl came over and said to him,
"You were one of those with Jesus the Galilean." But
Peter denied it in front of everyone. "I don't know
what you're talking about," he said. Later, out by the
gate, another servant girl noticed him and said to
those standing around, "This man was with Jesus of
Nazareth." Again Peter denied it, this time with an
oath. "I don't even know the man," he said. A little
later some of the other bystanders came over to Peter
and said, "You must be one of them; we can tell by
your Galilean accent." Peter swore, "A curse on me if
I'm lying—I don't know the man!" And immediately
the rooster crowed. Suddenly, Jesus' words flashed
through Peter's mind: "Before the rooster crows, you
will deny three times that you even know me." And
he went away, weeping bitterly.   Matthew 26:69-75

Jesus replied, "You are blessed. . . . Now I say to you
that you are Peter (which means 'rock'), and upon

this rock I will build my church, and all the powers of hell will not conquer it."   MATTHEW 16:17-18

This means that anyone who belongs to Christ has become a new person. The old life is gone; a new life has begun!   2 CORINTHIANS 5:17

If the memories and experiences of your life were compared to rocks that you have collected and must carry in a backpack, guilt and regret would be among the heaviest. Guilt is a legitimate spiritual response to sin. Regret is sorrow over the consequences of your decisions, both the sinful and the simply unfortunate. While God promises to remove the guilt of all who seek his forgiveness, he does not prevent the consequences of your sin. It is likely the regret over those consequences that you are carrying, and it weighs you down with remorse. God promises to help you deal with your regrets so you can move on to the future without carrying a heavy load of guilt. When you ask God for forgiveness, he promises to forget the past, and he gives you a fresh start. You still have to live with the consequences of your actions, because those cannot be retracted. But because God forgives and forgets, you can move forward without the heavy burden of regret. Because God no longer holds your past against you, you no longer need to hold it against yourself. You can be free from self-condemnation. Regrets can be so enslaving that they consume your thoughts and disable you from serving God in the future. If Peter had focused on the regret he experienced after denying Jesus, he would never have been able to preach the Good News so powerfully. Don't let regret paralyze you. Instead, let God's forgiveness motivate you to positive action for him in the future. It is a divine moment when you truly grasp the power of God's healing forgiveness and are able to turn your regrets into resolve.

DIVINE PROMISE

DAVID ALSO SPOKE OF THIS WHEN HE DESCRIBED THE HAPPINESS OF THOSE WHO ARE DECLARED RIGHTEOUS WITHOUT WORKING FOR IT: "OH, WHAT JOY FOR THOSE WHOSE DISOBEDIENCE IS FORGIVEN, WHOSE SINS ARE PUT OUT OF SIGHT. YES, WHAT JOY FOR THOSE WHOSE RECORD THE LORD HAS CLEARED OF SIN." *Romans 4:6-8*

Relationships

MY QUESTIONS *for* GOD

How can I feel closer to God? What can my other relationships teach me about intimacy with God?

A MOMENT *with* GOD

"When that day comes," says the LORD, "you will call me 'my husband' instead of 'my master.' . . . I will make you my wife forever, showing you righteousness and justice, unfailing love and compassion."

HOSEA 2:16, 19

See how very much our Father loves us, for he calls us
his children.   1 JOHN 3:1

Jesus replied, "The most important commandment
is this: 'Listen, O Israel! The LORD our God is the
one and only LORD. And you must love the LORD
your God with all your heart, all your soul, all your
mind, and all your strength.' The second is equally
important: 'Love your neighbor as yourself.' No
other commandment is greater than these."

MARK 12:29-31

There is no image that can completely express the
kind of relationship God wants to have with you. The
Bible uses the images of love between husband and
wife or father and child to give you some glimpse of it.
Your relationships are very important because as you
learn to relate to others, you learn how God designed
all relationships to work. Your relationship with God
is the most important relationship you have, although
this does not mean you should neglect your relationships with others. It is often through other people that
you learn about relating to God. It is through closeness with others that you learn how to be intimate,
how to share your heart and thoughts and dreams with
someone else. With God, you're already halfway there
because he knows your heart, your thoughts, your motives, your dreams. He wants to make you the best you
can be. He knows the best and the worst in you, and
he saved you anyway. When you accept that and start
to pursue closeness with God just as you would in any

other relationship, you will begin to know God intimately, and you will experience a loving relationship that no other can compare to.

DIVINE PROMISE

LONG AGO THE LORD SAID TO ISRAEL:
"I HAVE LOVED YOU, MY PEOPLE, WITH AN
EVERLASTING LOVE. WITH UNFAILING LOVE
I HAVE DRAWN YOU TO MYSELF." *Jeremiah 31:3*

Relevance

MY QUESTION *for* GOD

Is the Bible really relevant today?

A MOMENT *with* GOD

The grass withers and the flowers fade, but the word of our God stands forever.   ISAIAH 40:8

All Scripture is inspired by God and is useful to teach us what is true and to make us realize what is wrong in our lives. It corrects us when we are wrong and teaches us to do what is right. God uses it to prepare and equip his people to do every good work.

2 TIMOTHY 3:16-17

The Bible has stood the test of time better than any other document in human history. Over several centuries, God inspired a select number of people to write down what he wanted to reveal to us about himself and how he expects us to live. The events in the Bible were carefully recorded by eyewitnesses or people who knew the witnesses, and many of the events have been confirmed by secular historians through archeological findings. The Bible has been faithfully preserved because it is God's very words to us. He will not let them disappear from the face of the earth or allow them to be altered by human hands. The Bible applies to all generations, cultures, and social classes. And miraculously, it speaks to each of us individually as well. Because the Bible is the Word of God, it is the only document that is actually living. In other words, it is as contemporary as the heart of God and as relevant as your most urgent need. The Bible offers wisdom about everything, from the practical matters of daily life to the eternal matters of the heart. It is relevant because it gives you a picture of who your Creator is and what he has in store for you when you trust and follow him. No other book is as deeply life-changing as the Bible, the inspired Word of God. In it you will find a lifetime of divine moments.

DIVINE PROMISE

THE WORD OF GOD IS ALIVE AND POWERFUL.
IT IS SHARPER THAN THE SHARPEST
TWO-EDGED SWORD, CUTTING BETWEEN
SOUL AND SPIRIT, BETWEEN JOINT AND
MARROW. IT EXPOSES OUR INNERMOST
THOUGHTS AND DESIRES.   *Hebrews 4:12*

Repentance

MY QUESTIONS *for* GOD

What is repentance? What happens when I repent?

A MOMENT *with* GOD

There is forgiveness of sins for all who repent.

LUKE 24:47

Peter's words pierced their hearts, and they said to him and to the other apostles, "Brothers, what should we do?" Peter replied, "Each of you must repent of your sins and turn to God, and be baptized in the name of Jesus Christ for the forgiveness of your sins. Then you will receive the gift of the Holy Spirit."

ACTS 2:37-38

Now repent of your sins and turn to God, so that your sins may be wiped away.

ACTS 3:19

If my people who are called by my name will humble themselves and pray and seek my face and turn from their wicked ways, I will hear from heaven and will forgive their sins.

2 CHRONICLES 7:14

As you learned to drive, did you ever have the experience of suddenly realizing you were going the wrong way on a one-way street? What you do to correct your error is a good picture of the biblical idea of repentance. You make a U-turn and change your direction as fast as you can. Repentance is brought about when you realize that you are going the wrong way in life. The Bible calls this wrong way sin. Repentance is admitting your sin and making a commitment to change the direction of your life with God's help. While repentance is not a popular concept these days, it is essential because it is the only way to arrive at your desired destination—heaven. Repentance makes change possible so you can experience God's fullest blessings, both now and for eternity. Repentance is that divine moment where you decide to move toward God instead of away from him. Are you going in the right direction?

DIVINE PROMISE

COME BACK TO ME, AND I WILL HEAL YOUR WAYWARD HEARTS. *Jeremiah 3:22*

Reputation

MY QUESTION *for* GOD

Is a good reputation kind of overrated?

A MOMENT *with* GOD

"Here I am, a stranger and a foreigner among you. Please sell me a piece of land so I can give my wife a proper burial." The Hittites replied to Abraham, "Listen, my lord, you are an honored prince among us. Choose the finest of our tombs and bury her there. No one here will refuse to help you in this way."

GENESIS 23:4-6

$\mathcal{L}$ike it or not, you already have a reputation. Whether you intentionally try to project a certain image or you couldn't care less what others think, people still form an opinion of you based on what you do and say. Abraham's reputation earned him respect even among strangers. Reputation is the yardstick that others use to measure your character. Take a moment to imagine what others might say about you. How would they describe your reputation? A life invested in obedience to God results in a reputation that brings honor and respect.

DIVINE PROMISE

CHOOSE A GOOD REPUTATION OVER GREAT RICHES; BEING HELD IN HIGH ESTEEM IS BETTER THAN SILVER OR GOLD.   *Proverbs 22:1*

Respect

MY QUESTIONS *for* GOD

Where can I find a little respect these days? What does God say about getting respect?

A MOMENT *with* GOD

Whoever wants to be a leader among you must be your servant.   MATTHEW 20:26

I pressed further, "What you are doing is not right!"
                                                        NEHEMIAH 5:9

He must become greater and greater, and I must
become less and less.

JOHN 3:30

*T*he keys to earning respect may not be what you expect. Respect comes from serving rather than being
served. Respect comes from taking responsibility for
your actions rather than trying to save face in front of
others. Respect comes from speaking up when things
are wrong rather than going along with the crowd. Respect comes from building others up rather than making yourself look good. The world says you need to look
like a model and act cool, to speak with irreverence
and to do only what's best for yourself. In the end,
this self-centered standard of living will only bring you
down in the eyes of your peers. These things promise
respect, but they only make you look "cool." The problem with cool is that it only lasts until something or
someone else is more cool. Trying to be cool just sets
you up for failure. True respect is reserved for people
who consistently live a life of kindness and integrity,
and are motivated by a deep love for others. As God becomes greater and greater in your life, you will become
the kind of person who truly deserves respect.

DIVINE PROMISE

THERE WILL BE GLORY AND HONOR AND PEACE
FROM GOD FOR ALL WHO DO GOOD. *Romans 2:10*

Responsibility

MY QUESTION for GOD

How does being responsible reflect my trust in God?

A MOMENT with GOD

Potiphar gave Joseph complete administrative responsibility over everything he owned. . . . With Joseph there, he didn't worry about a thing.

GENESIS 39:4-6

If you see that your neighbor's donkey or ox has collapsed on the road, do not look the other way. Go and help your neighbor get it back on its feet!

DEUTERONOMY 22:4

Don't excuse yourself by saying, "Look, we didn't know."

PROVERBS 24:12

Even as a slave, Joseph was put in charge of Potiphar's entire household. When he was thrown into prison, the prison warden put Joseph in charge of all the prisoners. Both Potiphar and the prison warden clearly saw that Joseph was a responsible person. To be responsible, you must be able to discern what needs to be done and then follow through to see that it happens. You can be depended upon to be where you are supposed to be when you are supposed to be there, and to be consistent in what you say and do. Those who follow God should be more responsible than those who don't because they should display godly character traits. Responsibility also opens doors of opportunity. How you handle each responsibility determines whether or not you will be trusted with more.

DIVINE PROMISE

TO THOSE WHO USE WELL WHAT THEY ARE GIVEN, EVEN MORE WILL BE GIVEN, AND THEY WILL HAVE AN ABUNDANCE. BUT FROM THOSE WHO DO NOTHING, EVEN WHAT LITTLE THEY HAVE WILL BE TAKEN AWAY. *Matthew 25:29*

Rest

MY QUESTION *for* GOD

How can rest allow me to experience more of life?

A MOMENT *with* GOD

The creation of the heavens and the earth and everything in them was completed. On the seventh day God had finished his work of creation, so he rested from all his work. And God blessed the seventh day and declared it holy, because it was the day when he rested from all his work of creation.

GENESIS 2:1-3

It is useless for you to work so hard from early morning until late at night, anxiously working for food to eat; for God gives rest to his loved ones.

PSALM 127:2

Then Jesus said, "Let's go off by ourselves to a quiet place and rest awhile." He said this because there were so many people coming and going that Jesus and his apostles didn't even have time to eat.   MARK 6:31

God wants you to take a break and get some rest. He set aside a full day of rest after his work of creation as an example for you to follow. God probably didn't have to rest, but he understands the balance between hard work and refreshment. Jesus also understood the needs and limitations of his disciples and took them away for a break. Work is good, but it must be balanced by rest. While all-night study sessions and long hours of doing homework may sometimes be necessary, it is equally necessary to take a break in order to refresh your mind, your body, and your spirit. A full life comes from work *and* rest. Only through rest is it possible to be relaxed enough to experience divine moments of enjoyment that can refresh you and inspire you in your work.

DIVINE PROMISE

THERE IS A SPECIAL REST STILL WAITING FOR THE PEOPLE OF GOD. FOR ALL WHO HAVE ENTERED INTO GOD'S REST HAVE RESTED FROM THEIR LABORS, JUST AS GOD DID AFTER CREATING THE WORLD.   *Hebrews 4:9-10*

Rewards

MY QUESTION *for* GOD

Are there rewards for obeying God?

A MOMENT *with* GOD

That day Moses solemnly promised me, "The land of Canaan on which you were just walking will be your grant of land and that of your descendants forever, because you wholeheartedly followed the LORD my God."

JOSHUA 14:9

There truly is a reward for those who live for God; surely there is a God who judges justly here on earth.

PSALM 58:11

The LORD rewarded me for doing right. He has seen my innocence. To the faithful you show yourself faithful; to those with integrity you show integrity. To the pure you show yourself pure, but to the wicked you show yourself hostile. 2 SAMUEL 22:25-27

There are definitely rewards for obeying God, as Caleb discovered. Because Caleb wholeheartedly obeyed the Lord, he was rewarded with land. This is an example of how obeying God brings both earthly and heavenly rewards. For example, obeying God often protects you from evil that God knows is there; it leads you on the right paths to find more of God's blessings; and it directs you into service that will please God and help others. It sometimes results in material rewards, but not always. The principle that God rewards obedience still applies today, but you must not expect your rewards to involve possessions or earthly prosperity. Instead, you should expect your rewards to involve spiritual prosperity—the marvelous gifts of salvation and eternal life, the blessings of a relationship with the Creator of the universe, the treasure of God's Word, and the wonderful character traits of godliness, truth, wisdom, and a good reputation. These are rewards that are lasting and priceless, and God promises them to you when you follow him.

DIVINE PROMISE

THE LORD WILL WITHHOLD NO GOOD THING
FROM THOSE WHO DO WHAT IS RIGHT.
Psalm 84:11

Risks

MY QUESTION *for* GOD

How do I decide when to live it up and when to play it safe?

A MOMENT *with* GOD

Be careful then, dear brothers and sisters. Make sure that your own hearts are not evil and unbelieving, turning you away from the living God.   HEBREWS 3:12

Listen, O Israel! The LORD is our God, the LORD
alone. And you must love the LORD your God with
all your heart, all your soul, and all your strength.

DEUTERONOMY 6:4-5

Faith is the confidence that what we hope for will
actually happen; it gives us assurance about things we
cannot see. Through their faith, the people in days of
old earned a good reputation. . . . It was by faith that
Noah built a large boat to save his family from the
flood. . . . It was by faith that Abraham obeyed when
God called him to leave home and go to another
land that God would give him as his inheritance.
. . . Abraham was confidently looking forward to a
city with eternal foundations.   HEBREWS 11:1-2, 7-10

"*Be careful crossing the street!*" "Be careful with the
car!" "Just be careful!" Your parents are always warning you about the risks of certain behaviors. God, your
heavenly father, also warns you to be careful about
what you do. His instructions are more along the lines
of "Be careful not to let your anger control you" or
"Use caution around ungodly people" or "Watch out!
Don't let your thoughts lead you into sin." God gives
you clear warnings in the Bible to guide you away from
risky behaviors that are potentially hurtful or destructive. But God also encourages you to take certain risks,
the kind that result in a godly life. It is in taking these
risks that God's Word tells you to go ahead and take
the plunge. For example, God might be saying, "Go
ahead, attend that college that keeps popping into your

mind." "Go on that missions trip." "Accept that job." "Help that person." "Accept that challenge." Taking such a risk means stepping out in faith to do the very thing God wants you to do. Taking risks that help you grow in your faith, and avoiding risks that harm your walk with God, will ensure that your life is a healthy and happy adventure. What a divine moment to take a risk and find that God is in it!

DIVINE PROMISE

COMMIT EVERYTHING YOU DO TO THE LORD. TRUST HIM, AND HE WILL HELP YOU.   *Psalm 37:5*

Romance

MY QUESTIONS *for* GOD

Is it wrong to want to find someone to share my life with? How do I find the right person?

A MOMENT *with* GOD

For everything there is a season, a time for every activity under heaven. . . . A time to embrace and a time to turn away.   ECCLESIASTES 3:1, 5

Promise me, O women of Jerusalem, by the gazelles and wild deer, not to awaken love until the time is right.   SONG OF SONGS 2:7

*I*t's natural to want a romantic relationship—God created us to need other people. That desire is planted in every human heart, and it finds the most beautiful expression within the boundaries of a healthy marriage relationship. God made romance, so it is not a bad thing unless it is misused. One question to ask yourself is this: How badly do I want a romantic relationship? Do you want it so badly that you'll get involved with just anyone, regardless of God's standards? Good relationships with the opposite sex happen most naturally when you are not focusing on finding a boyfriend or a girlfriend. A good romantic relationship begins with friendship. It grows through shared values and experiences and the shared goal of loving and serving God for a lifetime. Pursue genuine friendships, including those with members of the opposite sex, and keep serving the God who loves you more deeply than any other friend. Your patience as you wait for God's perfect timing in the area of romance increases your capacity to love.

DIVINE PROMISE

MY FUTURE IS IN YOUR HANDS. *Psalm 31:15*

Sacrifice

MY QUESTION *for* GOD

How should I respond when people make sacrifices for me?

A MOMENT *with* GOD

Once during the harvest, when David was at the
cave of Adullam, the Philistine army was camped in
the valley of Rephaim. The Three (who were among
the Thirty—an elite group among David's fighting
men) went down to meet him there. David was
staying in the stronghold at the time, and a Philistine
detachment had occupied the town of Bethlehem.
David remarked longingly to his men, "Oh, how I
would love some of that good water from the well by
the gate in Bethlehem." So the Three broke through
the Philistine lines, drew some water from the well
by the gate in Bethlehem, and brought it back to
David. But he refused to drink it. Instead, he poured
it out as an offering to the LORD. "The LORD forbid
that I should drink this!" he exclaimed. "This water is
as precious as the blood of these men who risked their
lives to bring it to me." So David did not drink it.

                                                    2 SAMUEL 23:13-17

Let us offer through Jesus a continual sacrifice
of praise to God, proclaiming our allegiance to
his name.   HEBREWS 13:15

David's men risked their lives to bring him the fresh
water he longed for. David was so awed by their sacrifice that he could not drink it—he could not treat it as
just any cup of water. Because of the men's sacrifice,
the water became sacred to David. Don't trivialize the
sacrifices someone else makes for you. Parents may sacrifice a better lifestyle in order pay for your education,

or they may sacrifice their wants in order to supply your needs. Your friends might sacrifice their time to be with you or their reputation to defend you. Your teachers might sacrifice their free time in order to give you a little extra help outside of class. There are probably many people who make sacrifices for you. It's easy to be so busy or so preoccupied with your own needs that you take what they give without even acknowledging the cost. Instead you should have the kind of awe and gratitude that David showed. Pay attention to what people do for you, and take time to thank them for it. Snubbing sacrifice is most dangerous when it comes to responding to Jesus' death. He gave his very life so that you could live forever, yet how often do you respond with gratitude and awe? You can experience a divine moment in your life if you show the same respect for Jesus' death as David did for his men's risky venture.

DIVINE PROMISE

THIS IS REAL LOVE—NOT THAT WE LOVED GOD, BUT THAT HE LOVED US AND SENT HIS SON AS A SACRIFICE TO TAKE AWAY OUR SINS.   *1 John 4:10*

Salvation

MY QUESTION *for* GOD

How should my salvation affect my daily life?

A MOMENT *with* GOD

We know that our old sinful selves were crucified
with Christ so that sin might lose its power in our
lives. We are no longer slaves to sin. For when we
died with Christ we were set free from the power of
sin. And since we died with Christ, we know we will
also live with him.   ROMANS 6:6-8

He has created us anew in Christ Jesus, so we can do
the good things he planned for us long ago.

ЕPHESIANS 2:10

Since we have been made right in God's sight by faith,
we have peace with God.   ROMANS 5:1

If someone were to guarantee you that if you worked
until retirement age, you would at that point inherit
several million dollars, more than likely it would
change the way you live right now! You would worry
less, be more confident, perhaps take greater risks, be
more generous, have greater peace of mind. You might
choose a career based on how much it fulfills you instead of how much money you could make. When you
receive salvation by accepting Jesus Christ as Lord, you
are guaranteed to inherit eternal life in heaven, with
everything you could want or need provided for you.
This inheritance should change the way you live now.
You are able to discover and take part in the plan that
God has for you. You can worry less and be confident
that nothing can harm your soul or your eternal future.
You can take some risks by stepping out in faith when

you think God is asking you to do something for him. You can be more generous and have peace of mind. Too often those who have salvation live as though they don't. Live as though your future holds everything you could ever want—it truly does.

DIVINE PROMISE

ANYONE WHO BELONGS TO CHRIST HAS BECOME A NEW PERSON. THE OLD LIFE IS GONE; A NEW LIFE HAS BEGUN!   *2 Corinthians 5:17*

Satisfaction

MY QUESTION *for* GOD

Why don't I ever feel satisfied with my life?

A MOMENT *with* GOD

No matter how much we see, we are never satisfied. No matter how much we hear, we are not content.
ECCLESIASTES 1:8

Listen to me, and you will eat what is good. You will enjoy the finest food.   ISAIAH 55:2

You don't have what you want because you don't ask God for it. And even when you ask, you don't get it because your motives are all wrong—you want only what will give you pleasure.   JAMES 4:2-3

The Holy Spirit produces this kind of fruit in our lives: love, joy, peace, patience, kindness, goodness, faithfulness, gentleness, and self-control.

GALATIANS 5:22-23

The voice said to me, "Son of man, eat what I am giving you—eat this scroll! Then go and give its message to the people of Israel." So I opened my mouth, and he fed me the scroll. "Fill your stomach with this," he said. And when I ate it, it tasted as sweet as honey in my mouth. . . . Then he added, "Son of man, let all my words sink deep into your own heart first. Listen to them carefully for yourself."

EZEKIEL 3:1-3, 10

❧

Too many people try to meet their deepest needs in ways that just don't satisfy. When you are hungry, your body craves good food. If you eat only junk food, it will never truly satisfy your cravings. You'll get shaky, you won't be able to think straight, and your body won't function properly. If you make a habit of eating junk food instead of something healthy, you'll suffer long-term physical damage. The same principle applies to satisfying the hunger in your soul. If you try to fill yourself only with fun, pleasure, and sin, you'll always be craving something more. You'll throw your soul out of whack, and it won't function right. You need a steady diet of soul food—eat up God's Word and thirst for time with him so his Holy Spirit can fill you with the things that will make you a strong and mature believer. Only God can truly satisfy your deepest cravings because he created you to be in relationship with him. When you have eaten well of what God offers, you will have the strength and wisdom to take advantage of the opportunities God sends your way. You can be sure that this satisfaction will actually last because it comes directly from God.

DIVINE PROMISE

HE SATISFIES THE THIRSTY AND FILLS THE HUNGRY WITH GOOD THINGS. *Psalm 107:9*

Seeking God

MY QUESTION *for* GOD

How do I find God? How can I seek out a relationship with him?

A MOMENT *with* GOD

My heart has heard you say, "Come and talk with me." And my heart responds, "LORD, I am coming."

PSALM 27:8

The LORD is close to all who call on him, yes, to all who call on him in truth.

PSALM 145:18

Come close to God, and God will come close to you.

JAMES 4:8

When you have a close friend, you do your best to stay in touch. You talk almost every day. You go out and do things together, or you just reminisce with each other about fond memories. It's no different with God. A relationship with God requires effort, activity, daily contact, and building memories. When you're seeking out a relationship with God, talk to him every day. Be open and honest, just as you would be with a close friend. Then take the time to listen. Allow a few moments each day for quality time with God. Express your concerns, talk about your future, or remember ways he's been with you and helped you in the past. Don't forget to ask him what he's doing, too, both around the world and in your life. Read his Word daily to open yourself up to what he might be saying to you. Remember that God is with you all day, every day. You can talk to him about everything that comes up at home, at work, and everywhere else. Share your thoughts, needs, and concerns with him as they arise. As you get to know God by spending time with him every day, you'll begin to find the relationship you desire. God promises that if you search for him, you will find him. You'll wonder how you ever got along without him!

DIVINE PROMISE

IF YOU SEEK HIM, YOU WILL FIND HIM.

1 Chronicles 28:9

Self-Control

MY QUESTION *for* GOD

How does self-control help me experience the best in life?

A MOMENT *with* GOD

The LORD God warned him, "You may freely eat the fruit of every tree in the garden—except the tree of the knowledge of good and evil. If you eat its fruit, you are sure to die."   GENESIS 2:16-17

You must always obey the LORD's commands and decrees that I am giving you today for your own good.   DEUTERONOMY 10:13

We will not boast about things done outside our area of authority. We will boast only about what has happened within the boundaries of the work God has given us, which includes our working with you.

                                                    2 CORINTHIANS 10:13

Guide my steps by your word, so I will not be overcome by evil.   PSALM 119:133

*I*n track and field, if a runner steps out of his lane during a race, he is disqualified. In soccer, if a player kicks the ball out-of-bounds, the other team gets it. When it comes to sports, we understand that boundaries are necessary to keep the game fair and orderly. They keep people from getting hurt, and they keep the game moving toward a specific goal. With no rules, the game just wouldn't make sense. It would be random and pointless. That is why athletes must train themselves to perform well within the boundaries of their sport—so they can accomplish victory the right way. This same principle holds true in everyday life. God gives you boundaries so that life makes sense. When you practice self-control and stay within those boundaries, you have purpose and direction. When you can't control yourself and you go "out-of-bounds," you are penalized—not because God wants to punish you but because those are the rules in life. Going out-of-bounds has consequences. The world works by the rules God set in place at creation. You can't change them, and if you could, life wouldn't be as fulfilling. Instead of seeing boundaries as negative, limiting your freedom, try to see them as useful, keeping life moving toward the ultimate victory God promises to everyone who plays the game well and lives by the rules. If you exercise self-control and remain within God's boundaries, you will win the race of life and receive the reward of eternal life with God.

DIVINE PROMISE

MAKE ME WALK ALONG THE PATH OF YOUR
COMMANDS, FOR THAT IS WHERE MY
HAPPINESS IS FOUND. *Psalm 119:35*

Serving

MY QUESTION *for* GOD

How does serving others show my love for God?

A MOMENT *with* GOD

Now, Israel, what does the LORD your God require of you? He requires only that you fear the LORD your God, and live in a way that pleases him, and love him and serve him with all your heart and soul.

DEUTERONOMY 10:12

You have been called to live in freedom, my brothers and sisters. But don't use your freedom to satisfy your sinful nature. Instead, use your freedom to serve one another in love.

GALATIANS 5:13

Among you it will be different. Whoever wants to be a leader among you must be your servant. . . . For even the Son of Man came not to be served but to serve others and to give his life as a ransom for many.

MATTHEW 20:26-28

If you give even a cup of cold water to one of the least of my followers, you will surely be rewarded.

MATTHEW 10:42

We usually think of love as a feeling, but the Bible teaches that love is really an action—doing something for someone else with no thought of getting anything in return. You show your love for God by actively seeking a

relationship with him, by obeying his Word, and by worshiping him. You also show your love for God by serving
others. Genuine love is demonstrated through acts of
kindness and service. It is the consistent and courageous
decision to give of yourself for the well-being of others.
It is your expression of gratitude for God's loving care.
When you realize how much God loves you, you are
compelled to show that love to others by serving them.

DIVINE PROMISE

HE WILL NOT FORGET . . . HOW YOU HAVE
SHOWN YOUR LOVE TO HIM BY CARING FOR
OTHER BELIEVERS.   *Hebrews 6:10*

Sharing

MY QUESTION *for* GOD

Why should I share?

A MOMENT *with* GOD

There's a young boy here with five barley loaves and
two fish. But what good is that with this huge crowd?

JOHN 6:9

I always thank my God for you and for the gracious
gifts he has given you.   1 CORINTHIANS 1:4

As each part does its own special work, it helps the
other parts grow, so that the whole body is healthy
and growing and full of love.   EPHESIANS 4:16

*E*ver since we were little children, we've been taught
to share. Yet for most of us, it remains as hard as ever
to share either our things or ourselves. Why? Because
at the very core of our sinful human nature is the desire to get, not give; to accumulate, not relinquish; to
look out for ourselves, not for others. The Bible calls
you to share many things—your resources, your faith,
your love, your time, your talents, your money. Many
things, in fact, are more fully enjoyed when shared
with others. When you share, it benefits others far
more than you may realize. The boy in John 6 shared
his lunch, and Jesus multiplied it to feed thousands of
hungry people, allowing them to stay longer to hear his
message. Many people went home as believers because
of this extra time with Jesus. Five thousand people
were blessed by this one selfless act. Like the boy who
shared his lunch, you are called to share because God
shares so generously with you. Sharing is an expression of your love for God and for others. God has given
you special gifts and resources, and by sharing them
with others, you pass on what you have and multiply
God's blessings to others. Those who generously share
discover that the benefits of giving are far greater than
the temporary satisfaction of receiving.

DIVINE PROMISE

MAY YOU BE FILLED WITH JOY, ALWAYS
THANKING THE FATHER. HE HAS ENABLED
YOU TO SHARE IN THE INHERITANCE THAT
BELONGS TO HIS PEOPLE, WHO LIVE IN
THE LIGHT. *Colossians 1:11-12*

Sin

MY QUESTIONS *for* GOD

Isn't sin kind of an outdated word? What is sin anyway?

A MOMENT *with* GOD

All have turned away; all have become useless. No
one does good, not a single one.   ROMANS 3:12

When you follow the desires of your sinful nature,
the results are very clear: sexual immorality,
impurity, lustful pleasures, idolatry, sorcery,
hostility, quarreling, jealousy, outbursts of anger,
selfish ambition, dissension, division, envy,
drunkenness.   GALATIANS 5:19-21

Remember, it is sin to know what you ought to do
and then not do it.   JAMES 4:17

The words you speak come from the heart—that's
what defiles you. For from the heart come evil
thoughts, murder, adultery, all sexual immorality,
theft, lying, and slander.   MATTHEW 15:18-19

Everyone has sinned; we all fall short of God's
glorious standard.   ROMANS 3:23

Sin will always be an offensive word. We can talk
openly and impersonally about crimes like rape and
murder; we can calculate statistics about adultery,
unwed mothers, and divorce; we can trivialize greed,
selfishness, and lust (or even raise them up as cultural
values)—but to call anything sin makes us uncomfort-
able. The word *sin* implies the violation of an objective,
absolute standard of behavior established by God. We
almost instinctively feel like this is an infringement on
our rights. Yet that reaction displays a terrible mis-
understanding of sin and an underestimation of God.
When a doctor correctly diagnoses a disease in your
body, you do not accuse him of impinging on your freedom; rather, you are grateful because he can treat the
disease before it destroys your life. The Bible teaches
that sin is a disease of the soul. It will destroy your life
and lead to spiritual death if you do not treat it. God's
standards of behavior are like preventative medicine;
he prescribes them not to limit your freedom but to
curtail the disease of sin. Not only is the antidote for
sin free, but it also comes with the gift of eternal life.

DIVINE PROMISE

IF WE CONFESS OUR SINS TO HIM, HE IS
FAITHFUL AND JUST TO FORGIVE US OUR SINS
AND TO CLEANSE US FROM ALL WICKEDNESS.

1 John 1:9

Sorrow

MY QUESTION *for* GOD

What can I do when sorrow overwhelms me?

A MOMENT *with* GOD

My soul is crushed with grief to the point of death.

MARK 14:34

Weeping may last through the night, but joy comes with the morning.   PSALM 30:5

You will grieve, but your grief will suddenly turn to wonderful joy.   JOHN 16:20

Let's not get tired of doing what is good. At just the right time we will reap a harvest of blessing if we don't give up.   GALATIANS 6:9

Sorrow is one of the common denominators of human experience. It is guaranteed. Whether it is a result of the loss of a pet in childhood, the loss of innocence through abuse or neglect, or the loss of a parent, friend, or acquaintance, you will experience sorrow. Whether predictable and necessary or random and tragic, the things that cause you sorrow will affect you profoundly for the rest of your life. The Bible acknowledges that sorrow and grief are part of life, even for those who love God. When you feel discouraged, it is easy to turn inward and become paralyzed by your sadness and pain. But every day God opens doors of opportunity to help you cope with and eventually overcome your sorrow: helping someone in need, volunteering for a good cause, writing a note of encouragement to someone in worse circumstances than your own. These opportunities help you to look up from your own pain long enough to notice God's comforting presence all around you. Take comfort in the Bible's promises that sorrow won't get the last word. God will redeem your sorrow with his promises of comfort and hope.

DIVINE PROMISE

HE WILL WIPE EVERY TEAR FROM THEIR EYES, AND THERE WILL BE NO MORE DEATH OR SORROW OR CRYING OR PAIN. ALL THESE THINGS ARE GONE FOREVER. *Revelation 21:4*

Spiritual Dryness

MY QUESTION *for* GOD

Why can't I always maintain my enthusiasm for serving God?

A MOMENT *with* GOD

The seed on the rocky soil represents those who hear the message and immediately receive it with joy. But since they don't have deep roots, they don't last long. They fall away as soon as they have problems or are persecuted for believing God's word. MATTHEW 13:20-21

You must warn each other every day, while it is still
"today," so that none of you will be deceived by sin
and hardened against God.   HEBREWS 3:13

Scorching temperatures, blazing sun, and too many
days without rain will bring a drought. Plants wilt,
streams dry up—everything is thirsty. You've probably
experienced that parched feeling, when all you long
for is a cup of cold water. Your soul can become dry,
too, thirsting for something that will be truly fulfilling.
Seasons of drought can come upon your soul when you
experience the blazing pressures of life or the heat of
temptation. Your desire to know God and serve him
wilts and dries up. Just as a farmer must take extra
care of his fields in a drought, so you must take care
of your soul during times of spiritual dryness. Keep
watering it with God's Word, and God will revive you
with a sense of renewed purpose. Just as God sends the
rain to refresh the earth, he also sends opportunities
to revive your passion and purpose for him. When you
see the chance to refresh your soul, act immediately to
avoid unnecessary damage to your faith. When you get
serious about your faith, your enthusiasm for God will
grow by leaps and bounds. To protect your soul from
the dangers of drought, read God's Word daily, study
it, and refuse to be deceived by sin. Keep your focus
on serving Jesus Christ. As you persevere, God will
reward you with a divine moment of more joy than you
ever thought possible.

DIVINE PROMISE

THE LORD WILL GUIDE YOU CONTINUALLY,
GIVING YOU WATER WHEN YOU ARE DRY
AND RESTORING YOUR STRENGTH. YOU WILL
BE LIKE A WELL-WATERED GARDEN, LIKE AN
EVER-FLOWING SPRING.   *Isaiah 58:11*

Spiritual Gifts

MY QUESTIONS *for* GOD

What are spiritual gifts? How do I find out what mine are?

A MOMENT *with* GOD

The LORD said to Moses, "Look, I have specifically
chosen Bezalel son of Uri, grandson of Hur, of the
tribe of Judah. I have filled him with the Spirit of
God, giving him great wisdom, ability, and expertise
in all kinds of crafts. He is a master craftsman, expert
in working with gold, silver, and bronze. He is skilled
in engraving and mounting gemstones and in carving
wood. He is a master at every craft!"   EXODUS 31:1-5

In his grace, God has given us different gifts for
doing certain things well. So if God has given you
the ability to prophesy, speak out with as much faith
as God has given you. If your gift is serving others,
serve them well. If you are a teacher, teach well. If
your gift is to encourage others, be encouraging. If
it is giving, give generously. If God has given you
leadership ability, take the responsibility seriously.

And if you have a gift for showing kindness to others,
do it gladly.   ROMANS 12:6-8

*Y*our talents and abilities are not random or acciden-
tal; they are part of the unique way God has designed
you. God gave Bezalel talent as a craftsman and com-
missioned him to create beautiful objects for the Tab-
ernacle. God does his work on earth through people,
so he gives each of us special gifts and talents. These
abilities may someday become your full-time job, or
they may simply be hobbies. Either way, God wants you
to use them. It is exciting and deeply satisfying to serve
God by doing the things you enjoy. Do you know the
unique gifts God has given you? If not, find out! Take
a spiritual gifts assessment, or ask your friends what
they think your gifts are. God gives each individual a
spiritual gift (sometimes more than one) and a special
ministry in the church for using those gifts to help and
encourage others and bring glory to his name. When
you use your spiritual gifts, you will fulfill the purpose
for which God made you. You can never use up these
spiritual gifts; rather, the more you use them, the more
they will be developed and allow you to make a unique
contribution in your sphere of influence. Using your
spiritual gifts creates divine moments when you find
the sweet spot of your effectiveness for God.

DIVINE PROMISE

GOD HAS GIVEN EACH OF YOU A GIFT FROM
HIS GREAT VARIETY OF SPIRITUAL GIFTS. USE
THEM WELL TO SERVE ONE ANOTHER. DO YOU
HAVE THE GIFT OF SPEAKING? THEN SPEAK
AS THOUGH GOD HIMSELF WERE SPEAKING
THROUGH YOU. DO YOU HAVE THE GIFT
OF HELPING OTHERS? DO IT WITH ALL THE
STRENGTH AND ENERGY THAT GOD SUPPLIES.
THEN EVERYTHING YOU DO WILL BRING
GLORY TO GOD THROUGH JESUS CHRIST.
ALL GLORY AND POWER TO HIM FOREVER
AND EVER! AMEN.   *1 Peter 4:10-11*

Spiritual Warfare

MY QUESTIONS *for* GOD

Is spiritual warfare real? If so, how do I fight?

A MOMENT *with* GOD

We are not fighting against flesh-and-blood enemies,
but against evil rulers and authorities of the unseen
world, against mighty powers in this dark world, and
against evil spirits in the heavenly places.

EPHESIANS 6:12

Jesus told him, "No! The Scriptures say, 'People do
not live by bread alone, but by every word that comes
from the mouth of God.'" . . . Jesus responded, "The
Scriptures also say, 'You must not test the LORD your
God.'" . . . "Get out of here, Satan," Jesus told him.

"For the Scriptures say, 'You must worship the LORD your God and serve only him.'"

MATTHEW 4: 4, 7, 10

Take the sword of the Spirit, which is the word of God.

EPHESIANS 6:17

The Bible clearly teaches that we are involved in a spiritual battle. Far from excluding you from this spiritual battle, faith puts you right in the middle of it. You are in a battle for your soul. You must recognize this and arm yourself, or you will be defeated. Your best offensive weapon in spiritual warfare is the Word of God. In the Bible, God reveals his plan of attack against evil. It's your battle plan; if you don't read it, you won't know how to fight the battle that determines your present and eternal destiny. Only by knowing who you are fighting, where the battle is, and how to defend yourself will you be able to win. The Bible exposes the enemy, Satan, for who he is. It shines the light of truth on his lies, teaches you how to prepare for his attacks, and gives you wisdom to fight his tricks and strategies. It is vital to read God's Word regularly because it is the only weapon that will send Satan running for cover.

DIVINE PROMISE

THE LORD IS FAITHFUL; HE WILL STRENGTHEN YOU AND GUARD YOU FROM THE EVIL ONE.

2 Thessalonians 3:3

Strengths and Weaknesses

MY QUESTION *for* GOD

What is true strength and weakness in the eyes of God?

A MOMENT *with* GOD

If I could speak all the languages of earth and of angels, but didn't love others, I would only be a noisy gong or a clanging cymbal. If I had the gift of prophecy, and if I understood all of God's secret plans and possessed all knowledge, and if I had such faith that I could move mountains, but didn't love others, I would be nothing. If I gave everything I have to the poor and even sacrificed my body, I could boast about it; but if I didn't love others, I would have gained nothing.   1 CORINTHIANS 13:1-3

Keep watch and pray, so that you will not give in to temptation. For the spirit is willing, but the body is weak!   MATTHEW 26:41

God has not given us a spirit of fear and timidity, but of power, love, and self-discipline.   2 TIMOTHY 1:7

It is a common misconception that following God means being weak. On the contrary, it takes strength to humbly obey God when you are tempted to sin. It takes great courage to serve others through acts of kindness when you don't feel like it. On the other hand, don't mistake power for true strength. Power tries to control; strength tries to love, no matter what. The biblical concept of strength is power under the control of love.

Each time he said, "My grace is all you need.
My power works best in weakness." So now I am glad
to boast about my weaknesses, so that the power of
Christ can work through me.   2 CORINTHIANS 12:9

*S*pecial abilities do not always make you strong. In
fact, the challenges, complexities, and demands of
life often reveal your weaknesses. But God's wisdom
and power are demonstrated even better through your
weaknesses than through your so-called strengths.
True weakness is depending on your own strength.
True strength comes when you see your weaknesses as
opportunities to allow God's power to work through
you. Divine moments come when you experience
God's power working through your weaknesses to
make you stronger.

DIVINE PROMISE

THAT'S WHY I TAKE PLEASURE IN MY
WEAKNESSES, AND IN THE INSULTS,
HARDSHIPS, PERSECUTIONS, AND TROUBLES
THAT I SUFFER FOR CHRIST. FOR WHEN I AM
WEAK, THEN I AM STRONG.   *2 Corinthians 12:10*

Stress

MY QUESTION *for* GOD

How should I cope when I am under stress?

A MOMENT *with* GOD

The Israelites did evil in the LORD's sight. . . . They abandoned the LORD. . . . He turned them over to their enemies all around, and they were no longer able to resist them. Every time Israel went out to battle, the LORD fought against them, causing them to be defeated, just as he had warned. And the people were in great distress.   JUDGES 2:11-15

*C*ertain actions have predictable consequences. If you try to stop a speeding car with your bare hands, you will get run over. Of course, you would never do that. But the Bible talks about another kind of action that has a predictable consequence—sin. God's Word makes it clear that sin always hurts you. It separates you from God, the source of mercy and blessing, and puts you in the shadow of the enemy. Giving in to temptation will put you under stress because it puts you right in the middle of the road, where evil hurtles toward you at high speed. Being run over by the consequences of sin causes great strain and enormous complications in your life. Of course, not all stress is caused by sinful actions. But the next time you are really feeling stressed out, as the people of Israel were, you should first check your heart and your actions to see if there are areas of your life where you are giving in to sin. Then get off the road of temptation before the consequences of sin run you over. Return to the Lord, and ask for his help and mercy. God has a soft spot for humble and repentant people.

DIVINE PROMISE

I HAVE TOLD YOU ALL THIS SO THAT YOU
MAY HAVE PEACE IN ME. HERE ON EARTH YOU
WILL HAVE MANY TRIALS AND SORROWS.
BUT TAKE HEART, BECAUSE I HAVE OVERCOME
THE WORLD.   *John 16:33*

Stubbornness

MY QUESTION *for* GOD

How do I know if I am being stubborn?

A MOMENT *with* GOD

But no, my people wouldn't listen. Israel did not want
me around. So I let them follow their own stubborn
desires, living according to their own ideas.

PSALM 81:11-12

Pharaoh's heart, however, remained hard. He still
refused to listen, just as the LORD had predicted.

EXODUS 7:13

Be careful then, dear brothers and sisters. Make sure
that your own hearts are not evil and unbelieving,
turning you away from the living God. You must
warn each other every day, while it is still "today," so
that none of you will be deceived by sin and hardened
against God. For if we are faithful to the end, trusting
God just as firmly as when we first believed, we will
share in all that belongs to Christ.   HEBREWS 3:12-14

*Y*ou are being stubborn when you refuse to believe that Jesus can make a difference in your life. You are being stubborn when you allow difficult circumstances to convince you that God does not care; when you stop praying because you've made up your mind it won't help anyway; when you refuse to trust God and instead depend on your own strength. The worst kind of stubbornness is when you refuse to consider that following God's rules for living, as found in the Bible, will make your life better. You've got your plans, and you don't want to admit that God's plan for your life might actually be better. You'd have to give up certain habits and lifestyle choices, and you just don't want to go there. Let God break through the stubbornness. He can show you how to give up those things you think are so good and exchange them for things he knows are so much better. When you humble yourself to admit there might be a better way, not only will you experience a divine moment with God, but you'll have a breakthrough in your relationships with others, too.

DIVINE PROMISE

I WILL GIVE YOU A NEW HEART, AND I WILL
PUT A NEW SPIRIT IN YOU. I WILL TAKE OUT
YOUR STONY, STUBBORN HEART AND GIVE YOU
A TENDER, RESPONSIVE HEART. *Ezekiel 36:26*

Success

MY QUESTION *for* GOD

*Is it okay to be successful in this life? How does God
define success?*

A MOMENT *with* GOD

All too quickly the message is crowded out by the
worries of this life, the lure of wealth, and the desire
for other things.   MARK 4:19

Our goal is to please him. For we must all stand
before Christ to be judged. We will each receive
whatever we deserve for the good or evil we have
done in this earthly body.   2 CORINTHIANS 5:9-10

Jesus replied, "'You must love the LORD your God
with all your heart, all your soul, and all your mind.'
This is the first and greatest commandment."

MATTHEW 22:37-38

Commit your actions to the LORD, and your plans
will succeed.   PROVERBS 16:3

In this world success is usually defined by how much
we own and how much we achieve. According to God's
standards, success is measured not by material assets
but by spiritual assets; not by what you have but by
who you are; not by what you know but by who you
know. Some people are successful both by the world's
standards and by God's standards, and there is nothing
wrong with that. We get into trouble when we gain

material or worldly success at the expense of true success as God defines it. When you die, you will leave behind all your material assets; what you own here on earth has absolutely no eternal value. But how well you have succeeded in what God considers important counts in every way. Partnering with God in this life is the best way to ensure success in the next.

DIVINE PROMISE

STUDY THIS BOOK OF INSTRUCTION CONTINUALLY. MEDITATE ON IT DAY AND NIGHT SO YOU WILL BE SURE TO OBEY EVERYTHING WRITTEN IN IT. ONLY THEN WILL YOU PROSPER AND SUCCEED IN ALL YOU DO. THIS IS MY COMMAND—BE STRONG AND COURAGEOUS! DO NOT BE AFRAID OR DISCOURAGED. FOR THE LORD YOUR GOD IS WITH YOU WHEREVER YOU GO. *Joshua 1:8-9*

Suffering

MY QUESTION *for* GOD

Can any good come from suffering?

A MOMENT *with* GOD

We can rejoice, too, when we run into problems and trials, for we know that they help us develop endurance. And endurance develops strength of character.

ROMANS 5:3-4

We don't look at the troubles we can see now; rather, we fix our gaze on things that cannot be seen. For the things we see now will soon be gone, but the things we cannot see will last forever.   2 CORINTHIANS 4:18

All praise to God, the Father of our Lord Jesus Christ. God is our merciful Father and the source of all comfort. He comforts us in all our troubles so that we can comfort others. When they are troubled, we will be able to give them the same comfort God has given us.   2 CORINTHIANS 1:3-4

It only makes sense that we who live in such a pleasure-seeking society would try to avoid suffering at any cost. But it is through suffering, like other challenges, that you grow. No one likes pain or adversity because it challenges you physically, mentally, emotionally, and spiritually. But those who go through such taxing times become stronger and wiser for it. An athlete or musician will never achieve greatness without painful hours of practice. Likewise, you will never become strong and wise without being pushed, shoved, and hurt by life's troubles. God never wants to see you suffer, but he sometimes allows painful and difficult times in your life to strengthen your character and faith. God uses suffering to change your perspective and turn your thoughts heavenward, to strengthen your faith as you wait expectantly for his promises to come true. Often it is not until you reach the other side of suffering that you can appreciate the perspective and growth it achieved in you.

DIVINE PROMISE

IN HIS KINDNESS GOD CALLED YOU TO SHARE
IN HIS ETERNAL GLORY BY MEANS OF CHRIST
JESUS. SO AFTER YOU HAVE SUFFERED A LITTLE
WHILE, HE WILL RESTORE, SUPPORT, AND
STRENGTHEN YOU, AND HE WILL PLACE YOU
ON A FIRM FOUNDATION.   *1 Peter 5:10*

MY QUESTION *for* GOD

How can I help and comfort someone who is suffering?

A MOMENT *with* GOD

Going over to him, the Samaritan soothed his wounds
with olive oil and wine and bandaged them. Then he
put the man on his own donkey and took him to an
inn, where he took care of him.   LUKE 10:34

Share each other's burdens, and in this way obey the
law of Christ.
                                    GALATIANS 6:2

If one part suffers, all the parts suffer with it, and if
one part is honored, all the parts are glad.

                                    1 CORINTHIANS 12:26

Be happy with those who are happy, and weep with
those who weep.
                                    ROMANS 12:15

Suffering is a universal experience. Some suffering comes as a result of chance circumstances, such as a car accident that maims someone or an illness that ravages or even takes the life of a loved one. Some suffering happens because of neglect, such as failure to prepare for difficult times. Sometimes suffering comes because you choose it, such as when you willingly take on enormous responsibilities in order to achieve a certain goal. Other times suffering comes from sin, such as when you deliberately go against God's commands and then suffer the consequences. Whatever the source, at some point everyone falls under the dark shadow of suffering. You won't always be able to explain it, but maybe the divine moment is realizing that you don't have to explain it. We don't usually know why suffering has come into the life of a certain person, and trying to explain it doesn't help. Remind yourself of two important aspects of suffering—it hurts, but then it helps when it brings comfort to others. Suffering enables a person to comfort others, which becomes a divine moment for everyone. When you join in someone else's suffering, you choose to be wounded along with them. When others are hurting, suffer along with them to bring them—and you—comfort and hope.

DIVINE PROMISE

ALL PRAISE TO GOD, THE FATHER OF OUR LORD JESUS CHRIST. GOD IS OUR MERCIFUL FATHER AND THE SOURCE OF ALL COMFORT. HE COMFORTS US IN ALL OUR TROUBLES SO THAT WE CAN COMFORT OTHERS. WHEN THEY ARE

TROUBLED, WE WILL BE ABLE TO GIVE THEM
THE SAME COMFORT GOD HAS GIVEN US.
2 Corinthians 1:3-4

Supernatural

MY QUESTION *for* GOD

Will I have supernatural abilities in heaven?

A MOMENT *with* GOD

Our bodies are buried in brokenness, but they will be
raised in glory. They are buried in weakness, but they
will be raised in strength. They are buried as natural
human bodies, but they will be raised as spiritual
bodies. For just as there are natural bodies, there are
also spiritual bodies. . . . Our physical bodies cannot
inherit the Kingdom of God. These dying bodies
cannot inherit what will last forever.

1 CORINTHIANS 15:43-44, 50

Do you ever wish you had superhuman abilities? This
desire may be more realistic than you ever thought.
After you die and Jesus comes again, your resurrected
body will be a physical body like the one you have now,
but it will also have supernatural characteristics. You
may be able to walk through walls, as Jesus did with his
resurrected body. More importantly, your new body
won't ever decay from the effects of sin. You will never
be sick or feel pain again, nor will your mind think

sinful thoughts. You will never again compare yourself to other people or wish that you were different. You will be fully and finally perfect in God's sight. The next time you wish for supernatural abilities, remember that what you're really longing for is life in heaven. Thank God for this divine reminder to look forward to your eternal future.

DIVINE PROMISE

OUR EARTHLY BODIES ARE PLANTED IN THE GROUND WHEN WE DIE, BUT THEY WILL BE RAISED TO LIVE FOREVER.   *1 Corinthians 15:42*

Surprise

MY QUESTION *for* GOD

In what ways is God surprising?

A MOMENT *with* GOD

He has brought down princes from their thrones and exalted the humble.   LUKE 1:52

Just then his disciples came back. They were shocked to find him talking to a woman, but none of them had the nerve to ask, "What do you want with her?" or "Why are you talking to her?" The woman left her water jar beside the well and ran back to the village, telling everyone, "Come and see a man who told me everything I ever did! Could he possibly be the

Messiah?" So the people came streaming from the village to see him.

JOHN 4:27-30

He gave up his divine privileges; he took the humble position of a slave and was born as a human being. When he appeared in human form, he humbled himself in obedience to God and died a criminal's death on a cross. Therefore, God elevated him to the place of highest honor and gave him the name above all other names.

PHILIPPIANS 2:7-9

God often does the opposite of what we might expect. He chose David, the youngest son of Jesse rather than the oldest, to be king of Israel. He used a donkey to correct the pagan prophet Balaam. He took Saul, the most vicious opponent of the early church, and transformed him into Paul, the greatest and most courageous missionary of all time. He cared for and respected women at a time when they had no rights. He took the cross, an object of death and ultimate defeat, and made it the sign of victory over sin and death for all eternity. God's creativity and ingenuity knows no boundaries. Don't limit God to your own understanding and expectations. He wants to surprise you in ways that inspire your awe, love, gratitude, and joy. When something wonderful happens to you, do you attribute it to luck? Instead you should recognize that your good fortune as a divine moment from the hand of God. Only when you believe that God is acting on your behalf will your relationship with him grow deeper.

DIVINE PROMISE

COME AND SEE WHAT OUR GOD HAS DONE,
WHAT AWESOME MIRACLES HE PERFORMS
FOR PEOPLE! *Psalm 66:5*

Temptation

MY QUESTION *for* GOD

How can knowing my weaknesses help me stand strong against temptation?

A MOMENT *with* GOD

The LORD was with Joseph, so he succeeded in everything he did as he served in the home of his Egyptian master. Potiphar noticed this and realized that the LORD was with Joseph, giving him success in everything he did. This pleased Potiphar, so he soon made Joseph his personal attendant. He put him in charge of his entire household and everything he owned. . . . Joseph was a very handsome and well-built young man, and Potiphar's wife soon began to look at him lustfully. "Come and sleep with me," she demanded. But Joseph refused. "Look," he told her, "my master trusts me with everything in his entire household. No one here has more authority than I do. He has held back nothing from me except you, because you are his wife. How could I do such a wicked thing? It would be a great sin against God."

GENESIS 39:2-9

It's interesting that Joseph was tempted with the one thing he didn't have—a relationship with a woman. His brothers had stripped him of everything when they sold him into slavery—family, possessions, status. But he had remained faithful to God and regained good living conditions and authority in Potiphar's house. Yet he must have been lonely, and that is exactly where Satan struck. Satan offered Joseph the opportunity to ease that loneliness. Joseph was able to refuse the sexual advances of Potiphar's wife because he knew why, when, and how to say no. He had determined to live a godly life in Egypt, even though no one back home would know. The pressure you feel when you are tempted to sin can best be handled by acknowledging sin for what it is and diligently standing firm in your commitment to God before. Standing firm may mean avoiding areas of temptation or even fleeing from compromising situations. Always be aware that Satan strikes where you are weakest. That's why it's important to recognize where you are weak and vulnerable so you will not be surprised when temptation knocks at your door. Like Joseph, if you are watching for it and praying for the strength to resist it when it comes, you will be well prepared to say no.

DIVINE PROMISE

THE TEMPTATIONS IN YOUR LIFE ARE NO DIFFERENT FROM WHAT OTHERS EXPERIENCE. AND GOD IS FAITHFUL. HE WILL NOT ALLOW THE TEMPTATION TO BE MORE THAN YOU CAN STAND. WHEN YOU ARE TEMPTED, HE

WILL SHOW YOU A WAY OUT SO THAT YOU
CAN ENDURE.   *1 Corinthians 10:13*

Temptation

MY QUESTION *for* GOD

How can I have the power to resist temptation?

A MOMENT *with* GOD

The Spirit who lives in you is greater than the spirit
who lives in the world.   1 JOHN 4:4

Every child of God defeats this evil world, and we
achieve this victory through our faith. And who can
win this battle against the world? Only those who
believe that Jesus is the Son of God.   1 JOHN 5:4-5

The temptations in your life are no different from
what others experience. And God is faithful. . . .
When you are tempted, he will show you a way out
so that you can endure.   1 CORINTHIANS 10:13

Satan has the power to overwhelm you if it is just him
against you. But against Jesus, Satan becomes a coward.
When Jesus lives in you in the form of the Holy Spirit,
his power becomes available to you—and then it is Satan
who is overwhelmed. This gives you the advantage in
overcoming any temptation. The devil can tempt you,
but he cannot coerce you. He can dangle the bait in front
of you, but he cannot force you to take it. He will try

every trick in the book to make you think you're missing out, that you cannot and should not resist. But you
can break free from temptation when you change your
focus from what's in front of you to who is inside of you.
Then you can discern the difference between the lies of
the devil and the truth of God's Word, between what
seems right and what's really right. So instead of thinking about missing out on something, think about what
you'll be gaining by choosing God's way. You have far
more power available to you than you think. When you
arm yourself with God's Word and rely on the presence
of his Spirit within you, temptations can become divine
moments in which you experience the power of God
helping you resist.

DIVINE PROMISE

RESIST THE DEVIL, AND HE WILL FLEE
FROM YOU. *James 4:7*

Testing

MY QUESTION *for* GOD

Does God really test my faith?

A MOMENT *with* GOD

Jeremiah, I have made you a tester of metals, that you
may determine the quality of my people. JEREMIAH 6:27

Dear brothers and sisters, when troubles come your
way, consider it an opportunity for great joy. For you
know that when your faith is tested, your endurance
has a chance to grow. So let it grow, for when your
endurance is fully developed, you will be perfect and
complete, needing nothing.   JAMES 1:2-4

Remember how the LORD your God led you through
the wilderness for these forty years, humbling you
and testing you to prove your character, and to find
out whether or not you would obey his commands.

                                      DEUTERONOMY 8:2

As a student, you are tested regularly to see if you
are retaining and understanding the material you are
learning. Auto consumers routinely take test drives
to determine the quality of the vehicle they want to
purchase. Companies invest vast sums in testing new
products to guarantee they will perform as advertised.
In the same way, our character and spiritual commitment are tested by the fires of hardship, persecution,
and suffering. The Bible distinguishes between *temptation,* which Satan uses to lead us into sin, and *testing,*
which God uses to purify us and move us toward spiritual growth and maturity. Out of testing comes a more
committed faith. Just as your teachers test you so your
performance can be improved, God tests your faith to
strengthen you and help you accomplish everything he
wants you to do. When you feel like your faith is being
tested, see it as a divine moment when God is working in your life to get your attention, strengthen your

relationship with him, and increase your influence on those around you.

DIVINE PROMISE

THESE TRIALS WILL SHOW THAT YOUR FAITH IS GENUINE. *1 Peter 1:7*

Thankfulness

MY QUESTION *for* GOD

How does trusting God give me a spirit of gratitude?

A MOMENT *with* GOD

Then Moses led the people of Israel away from the Red Sea, and they moved out into the desert of Shur. They traveled in this desert for three days without finding any water. When they came to the oasis of Marah, the water was too bitter to drink. So they called the place Marah (which means "bitter"). Then the people complained and turned against Moses. "What are we going to drink?" they demanded. So Moses cried out to the LORD for help, and the LORD showed him a piece of wood. Moses threw it into the water, and this made the water good to drink.

EXODUS 15:22-25

*N*o sooner had the Israelites witnessed the miraculous parting of the Red Sea than they began to complain about contaminated drinking water. What would cause them to forget so quickly how God had just provided for them? They missed the connection between thankfulness and trust. Not only must you be grateful *for* something, but you should be grateful *to* someone for the blessings you are given. The Israelites were grateful for their deliverance from the Egyptian army, but they forgot about the One to whom they should be grateful! That made their gratitude short-lived. When you are grateful to God, you want to please him because of what he does for you. Nothing pleases God more than when you trust in his love and care for you. Thankfulness for some *thing* doesn't satisfy the heart, but gratitude to some *One* makes for a full and contented heart.

DIVINE PROMISE

GIVE THANKS TO THE LORD, FOR HE IS GOOD!
HIS FAITHFUL LOVE ENDURES FOREVER.
1 Chronicles 16:34

Thoughts

MY QUESTION *for* GOD

Does it matter what I think as long as I do the right thing?

A Moment *with* God

I say, anyone who even looks at a woman with lust has already committed adultery with her in his heart.

MATTHEW 5:28

It is what comes from inside that defiles you. For from within, out of a person's heart, come evil thoughts, sexual immorality, theft, murder, adultery, greed, wickedness, deceit, lustful desires, envy, slander, pride, and foolishness.

MARK 7:20-22

The human heart is the most deceitful of all things, and desperately wicked. Who really knows how bad it is?

JEREMIAH 17:9

*W*hat you think about doesn't just come from your mind but from your heart. Your thoughts tell you the condition of your heart because your every action begins as a thought. Left unchecked, wrong thoughts will eventually result in wrong actions. For example, if you think a lot about having sex with a certain person, your heart will begin to convince your mind that what you want to do is okay. The more you think about it, the more your heart will pull you in that direction. The Bible says that the heart is "desperately wicked." In other words, don't trust your emotions to tell you what is the right thing to do. Trust God's Word because it comes from God's heart, which is good and perfect. Your heart, your thoughts, and your actions are all tied up together. Losing control of one little thought can lead to great tragedy. Only the self-control that comes from knowing and following God's heart can help you tame this wild trio. When God controls your heart, your heart will inspire your mind to produce godly thoughts, which will produce godly actions. Your thoughts absolutely matter!

DIVINE PROMISE

GUARD YOUR HEART ABOVE ALL ELSE, FOR IT DETERMINES THE COURSE OF YOUR LIFE.
Proverbs 4:23

Time

MY QUESTION *for* GOD

How does putting God first help me manage my time?

A MOMENT *with* GOD

Remember to observe the Sabbath day by keeping it holy. You have six days each week for your ordinary work, but the seventh day is a Sabbath day of rest dedicated to the LORD your God. . . . For in six days the LORD made the heavens, the earth, the sea, and everything in them; but on the seventh day he rested. That is why the LORD blessed the Sabbath day and set it apart as holy.   EXODUS 20:8-11

He told them, "This is what the LORD commanded: Tomorrow will be a day of complete rest, a holy Sabbath day set apart for the LORD. So bake or boil

as much as you want today, and set aside what is left
for tomorrow."

EXODUS 16:23

*B*elieve it or not, the best way to find the time you
need is to devote more time to God. Then you will
know what he wants you to do so that you can avoid
what you should not do. Devoting time to God gives
you the opportunity to discover his priorities for you.
It allows you to focus only on what God is asking you
to do instead of trying to do everything.

DIVINE PROMISE

TEACH US TO REALIZE THE BREVITY OF LIFE, SO
THAT WE MAY GROW IN WISDOM. *Psalm 90:12*

Timing of God

MY QUESTION *for* GOD

What are the benefits of waiting for God's timing?

A MOMENT *with* GOD

I wait quietly before God, for my victory comes from
him. . . . Let all that I am wait quietly before God,
for my hope is in him.

PSALM 62:1, 5

I waited patiently for the LORD to help me, and he
turned to me and heard my cry.

PSALM 40:1

This is the plan: At the right time he will bring
everything together under the authority of Christ—
everything in heaven and on earth.   EPHESIANS 1:10

*H*ow we hate to wait! Even trivial delays like red
lights or slow checkout lines can make us edgy, even
angry. It can be especially frustrating when it seems
like God does not act, even though you have prayed and
prayed, and it seems obvious to you that you are praying for the right thing. God's timing is usually different
from yours. It's hard to accept that his timing is best for
you because you can't see what's up ahead. You want
what's best for you—but you want it *now*. The ability
to wait quietly for something is evidence that you have
a strong character because it shows you have faith that
God's way is best. When you are able to wait for God
to act without becoming restless or agitated, you show
that you fully trust his timing. As the old saying goes,
God is rarely early, but he's never late.

DIVINE PROMISE

REJOICE IN OUR CONFIDENT HOPE. BE PATIENT
IN TROUBLE, AND KEEP ON PRAYING.
Romans 12:12

Trust

MY QUESTION for GOD

How do I know if God is trustworthy?

A MOMENT with GOD

God's way is perfect. All the LORD's promises prove true. He is a shield for all who look to him for protection.

PSALM 18:30

God can be trusted to keep his promise. HEBREWS 10:23

The LORD is compassionate and merciful . . . filled with unfailing love.

PSALM 103:8

Your unfailing love, O LORD, is as vast as the heavens; your faithfulness reaches beyond the clouds. Your righteousness is like the mighty mountains, your justice like the ocean depths. You care for people and animals alike, O LORD. How precious is your unfailing love, O God! All humanity finds shelter in the shadow of your wings.

PSALM 36:5-7

When people consistently tell the truth, they are trustworthy. They can be counted on to do what they promise. How much more trustworthy is the One who created truth, who set the principles of moral law into motion? God not only created truth, he *is* truth. Truth is not just one of God's character traits but is the essence of who he is. God cannot lie or renege on a promise he's made—it's impossible. What God promises will always come true. Because he is eternal, his truth will last forever. Just as God is truth, he is also love. Like truth, love is not just one of his character traits but is the essence of who he is. God's love for you, therefore, is unconditional and can never be withdrawn. He loves you—always. Because of God's unending truth and unfailing love, you can trust him completely. You can trust that God's Son, Jesus, died to save you from your sins and rose again from the dead. You can trust that God has a plan for your life, that he wants to guide you toward what is best for you, and that he has a place prepared for you in heaven. When you understand how trustworthy God is, you can step out in faith and let him lead you wherever he wants to take you. Your doubts will turn into eager expectation for the adventures God has in store for you.

DIVINE PROMISE

JESUS CHRIST IS THE SAME YESTERDAY, TODAY, AND FOREVER. *Hebrews 13:8*

Truth

MY QUESTION *for* GOD

What is truth? Is anything really true anymore?

A MOMENT *with* GOD

In the beginning God created the heavens and the earth.

GENESIS 1:1

You are God, O Sovereign LORD. Your words
are truth.   2 SAMUEL 7:28

All Scripture is inspired by God and is useful to teach
us what is true and to make us realize what is wrong
in our lives. It corrects us when we are wrong and
teaches us to do what is right.   2 TIMOTHY 3:16

The instructions of the LORD are perfect, reviving
the soul. The decrees of the LORD are trustworthy,
making wise the simple.   PSALM 19:7

Jesus responded, " . . . I was born and came into the
world to testify to the truth. All who love the truth
recognize that what I say is true."   JOHN 18:37

Jesus told him, "I am the way, the truth, and the life.
No one can come to the Father except through me."

                                                JOHN 14:6

Few things impact our daily lives as much as the concept of truth. First, there's telling the truth. We gravi-
tate toward those who tell the truth because they are
honest and trustworthy. Without trust, relationships
fall apart. We have to be truthful if we want relationships to work, teams and organizations to work, and
government to work. Second, there's absolute truth.
This includes the fundamental principles of nature, sci-
ence, and human behavior that have been evident since
the beginning of time. For example, the truth (or law)
of gravity is that when you drop an object, it will fall.
A truth of mathematics is that two plus two equals four.

A truth of biology is that the right amounts of hydrogen and oxygen atoms make water molecules. A truth about life in general is that every person enters this world as a baby and someday exits this world through death. Only a fool would argue that these truths aren't valid. There is nothing any person can do to change these fundamental truths about how the world works. The Bible tells us there is a third kind of truth: spiritual truth. This includes moral and supernatural principles about human relationships with God and others that are absolute and constant despite our feelings and beliefs to the contrary. We humans have always wanted to determine this kind of truth for ourselves or to believe it doesn't exist at all. While this kind of truth may be more difficult to accept and discover, it is the one that will most affect the way you live here on earth as well as your eternal destiny. Just as you can't reject the truth about gravity and expect to function well in this world, so you can't reject the truth about God and how he has determined life should work and expect your future to turn out the way you want it to. It's wise to discover and study this truth because it so completely impacts the life of every human being. You are free to ignore truth if you choose, but you do so at your own risk, both now and for eternity.

DIVINE PROMISE

TRUTHFUL WORDS STAND THE TEST OF TIME, BUT LIES ARE SOON EXPOSED. *Proverbs 12:19*

Unity

MY QUESTIONS *for* GOD

How can I make peace with others? Is true unity possible?

A MOMENT *with* GOD

Make every effort to keep yourselves united in the Spirit, binding yourselves together with peace.

EPHESIANS 4:3

Search for peace, and work to maintain it.   PSALM 34:14

The body has many different parts, not just one part.

1 CORINTHIANS 12:14

One key to unity is celebrating each other's differences. It's not about everyone agreeing or having the same opinion. It's about taking people with different opinions and directing them all toward a common goal. God has made everyone unique, so we should expect differences of opinion. But God also tells us to be united, which means that our differences must serve a greater goal. We should work together to bring about thoughtful, well-developed plans. Unity is difficult to achieve if you are convinced that your opinion is the best and therefore someone else's opinion is not good enough. This mind-set keeps you from listening to new ideas that might actually improve your own opinions. Don't tune out a potential divine moment in which God can help you see how different colors create a richer painting. Celebrate and anticipate differences of opinion, and bring them together to accomplish the objective. Then you will experience the unity that God designed us to share and enjoy.

DIVINE PROMISE

YOU ARE ALL CHILDREN OF GOD THROUGH FAITH IN CHRIST JESUS. AND ALL WHO HAVE BEEN UNITED WITH CHRIST IN BAPTISM HAVE PUT ON CHRIST, LIKE PUTTING ON NEW CLOTHES. THERE IS NO LONGER JEW OR GENTILE, SLAVE OR FREE, MALE AND FEMALE. FOR YOU ARE ALL ONE IN CHRIST JESUS.
Galatians 3:26-28

Usefulness

MY QUESTION *for* GOD

How can God use me to display his power?

A MOMENT *with* GOD

I also pray that you will understand the incredible greatness of God's power for us who believe him. This is the same mighty power that raised Christ from the dead and seated him in the place of honor at God's right hand in the heavenly realms.

EPHESIANS 1:19-20

I work and struggle so hard, depending on Christ's mighty power that works within me.　COLOSSIANS 1:29

It is not that we think we are qualified to do anything
on our own. Our qualification comes from God.

2 CORINTHIANS 3:5

I will be present with you in spirit, and so will the
power of our Lord Jesus.   1 CORINTHIANS 5:4

I pray that from his glorious, unlimited resources
he will empower you with inner strength through
his Spirit.   EPHESIANS 3:16

We now have this light shining in our hearts, but
we ourselves are like fragile clay jars containing this
great treasure. This makes it clear that our great
power is from God, not from ourselves.

2 CORINTHIANS 4:7

Imagine experiencing the earth's strongest earthquake, tallest tsunami, wildest volcano, and most devastating hurricane—all at the same time. This cannot
even begin to compare to God's power! He is the creator of all these phenomena, and what is created is never
more powerful than the creator. This same God has the
power to calm the storms in your heart, to dry up a
flood of fear, to quench the lust for sin, and to control
the whirlwind of your life. You must put more trust in
God's power than your own. Thankfully, God's power
does not depend on human strength. In fact, your resources can get in the way if you rely on them instead
of on the Lord. God's power flows through you, especially your weaknesses, like an electric current flows
through a wire. The wire is simply a conductor; it has

no power in itself. But without the wire, the current doesn't go anywhere. God is looking for people who are willing to be wired for his service. If you are willing, the same power God used to create the world and defeat Satan will be available to you.

DIVINE PROMISE

ALL GLORY TO GOD, WHO IS ABLE, THROUGH HIS MIGHTY POWER AT WORK WITHIN US, TO ACCOMPLISH INFINITELY MORE THAN WE MIGHT ASK OR THINK.   *Ephesians 3:20*

Values

MY QUESTION *for* GOD

What is the benefit of having godly values?

A MOMENT *with* GOD

No one can serve two masters. For you will hate one and love the other; you will be devoted to one and despise the other. You cannot serve both God and money.   MATTHEW 6:24

Wherever your treasure is, there the desires of your heart will also be.   LUKE 12:34

Be on guard. Stand firm in the faith. Be courageous. Be strong.   1 CORINTHIANS 16:13

These were his instructions to them: "You must always act in the fear of the LORD, with faithfulness and an undivided heart."

2 CHRONICLES 19:9

How do you spend your free time? What kind of entertainment do you enjoy? Who are your best friends? What do you think about most? How do you spend your money? Your answers to these questions show what your values are. Whatever you consider important, useful, and worthwhile is what you value. You may have heard someone say, "She doesn't have any values." But such a statement is simply not true. Everyone has values, either good or bad. The problem comes when you don't have God's values but instead let the world's values shape you. Your values are clear to those around you because what you do, how you spend your time and money, and what you talk about show exactly what you value most. This is true even for God—what he does and says shows what he values most. For example, God made you in his own image, so he must value you highly! Your eternal future is so valuable to God that he sacrificed the life of his own Son so that you could live with him forever. Actions reveal values. What you do shows what you really believe—or better yet, who you really believe in. When your actions reveal your belief in God, you open the door for God's transforming love to break through into the lives of others.

DIVINE PROMISE

WHO MAY WORSHIP IN YOUR SANCTUARY,
LORD? WHO MAY ENTER YOUR PRESENCE ON
YOUR HOLY HILL? THOSE WHO LEAD BLAMELESS
LIVES AND DO WHAT IS RIGHT, SPEAKING THE
TRUTH FROM SINCERE HEARTS.   *Psalm 15:1-2*

Victory

MY QUESTION *for* GOD

What are some victories I can achieve on a daily basis?

A MOMENT *with* GOD

Abraham never wavered in believing God's promise.
In fact, his faith grew stronger, and in this he brought
glory to God.   ROMANS 4:20

These trials will show that your faith is genuine. It is
being tested as fire tests and purifies gold—though
your faith is far more precious than mere gold. So
when your faith remains strong through many trials,
it will bring you much praise and glory and honor
on the day when Jesus Christ is revealed to the
whole world.   1 PETER 1:7

I have discovered this principle of life—that when
I want to do what is right, I inevitably do what is
wrong. . . . Oh, what a miserable person I am! Who
will free me from this life that is dominated by sin
and death? Thank God! The answer is in Jesus Christ
our Lord. So you see how it is: In my mind I really

want to obey God's law, but because of my sinful
nature I am a slave to sin.   ROMANS 7:21, 24-25

*A*lthough final victory over sin and death is already
assured because of your faith in Jesus, you can apply that
victory to the daily issues and temptations of your life.
You do this by obeying God in the little things—what
you say, what you look at, how you react to others,
what you think about, whether you tell the truth or
not. It takes discipline to obey God in the little things;
each day you will face many small battles to accomplish
this. You do it not to earn salvation but to experience
the joy and victory God intends for you right now! As
you win the little battles, you will experience more
peace in your life. Every day you are bombarded with
emotions that could easily undermine your spiritual
strength. Obedience to God steadies your heart, even
in times of pain, confusion, loneliness, or distraction.
When problems and temptations arise, you will already
have the habit of focusing on how completely God provides for you instead of how easily those things can
defeat you. It is in moments when you lose your focus
that sin strikes and defeats. But obeying God in the
little things gives you daily victories that strengthen
your hope and endurance and bring you greater peace
of mind. Today's small victories are all you need right
now—just take it one day at a time.

DIVINE PROMISE

VICTORY COMES FROM YOU, O LORD. MAY YOU
BLESS YOUR PEOPLE.   *Psalm 3:8*

Vulnerability

MY QUESTION *for* GOD

Can I trust God with my deepest, darkest secrets?

A MOMENT *with* GOD

If we confess our sins to him, he is faithful and just
to forgive us our sins and to cleanse us from all
wickedness.   1 JOHN 1:9

Confess your sins to each other and pray for
each other.   JAMES 5:16

The word of God is alive and powerful. It is sharper
than the sharpest two-edged sword, cutting between
soul and spirit, between joint and marrow. It exposes
our innermost thoughts and desires. Nothing in all
creation is hidden from God. Everything is naked and
exposed before his eyes, and he is the one to whom
we are accountable.   HEBREWS 4:12-13

Search me, O God, and know my heart; test me and
know my anxious thoughts. Point out anything in
me that offends you, and lead me along the path of
everlasting life.   PSALM 139:23-24

*W*hat if others knew who you really are, deep down inside? Does the thought scare you, or would you be okay with it? Everyone has a need for intimate relationships, but you must choose carefully to whom you reveal your heart. Vulnerability occurs in only the most intimate relationships because it requires you to reveal your fears, hurts, doubts, and the darkest things in your life, the things you never want to come out in the open. You probably resist being vulnerable with God about your sins, especially the ones you don't want to give up. But vulnerability requires full disclosure, not hiding or covering up. It is only through vulnerability that we find true healing, restoration, renewal, and forgiveness. It is only through vulnerability that you can experience a breakthrough in your relationship with God. When you confess your sin, seek forgiveness, and commit yourself to following God's ways, your relationship with God and with others will be restored; a great weight will be lifted from you. When you are vulnerable with God, his forgiveness breaks you free of your sinful way of life and his divine healing ushers you into a life of steady godliness. Then you will have the desire and the confidence to be vulnerable with God as well as others. You have nothing to fear, nothing to hide, because God knows you and forgives you.

DIVINE PROMISE

NOW THERE IS NO CONDEMNATION FOR THOSE WHO BELONG TO CHRIST JESUS. AND BECAUSE YOU BELONG TO HIM, THE POWER OF THE

LIFE-GIVING SPIRIT HAS FREED YOU FROM THE
POWER OF SIN THAT LEADS TO DEATH.

Romans 8:1-2

Warnings

MY QUESTION *for* GOD

How should I view God's warnings?

A MOMENT *with* GOD

You must warn each other every day, while it is still
"today," so that none of you will be deceived by sin
and hardened against God. . . . Remember what it
says: "Today when you hear his voice, don't harden
your hearts as Israel did when they rebelled."

HEBREWS 3:13-15

The laws of the LORD are true; each one is fair. They
are more desirable than gold, even the finest gold.
They are sweeter than honey, even honey dripping
from the comb. They are a warning to your servant, a
great reward for those who obey them.   PSALM 19:9-11

To whom can I give warning? Who will listen when
I speak? Their ears are closed, and they cannot hear.
They scorn the word of the LORD. They don't want
to listen at all.   JEREMIAH 6:10

Life is full of warnings. A red light at an intersection
warns you to stop. A poison label warns you to put that

product out of the reach of children. An ambulance siren warns you to get out of the way. How you view these warnings is a matter of perspective. You can look at them as intrusions that prevent you from enjoying life, or you can look at them as blessings that protect you so you can enjoy life more. God's warnings are designed to protect his people from the consequences of foolish actions. For example, God's warning to avoid sexual immorality prevents you from the possibility of a broken heart, an unplanned pregnancy, or a sexually transmitted disease. All too often we view these warnings as obstacles to our freedom. When we do that, we rebel against the very things that are designed to protect us. God's warnings are his way of trying to save you from doing something you'll later regret.

DIVINE PROMISE

IF YOU LISTEN TO THESE COMMANDS OF THE
LORD YOUR GOD THAT I AM GIVING YOU
TODAY, AND IF YOU CAREFULLY OBEY THEM,
THE LORD WILL MAKE YOU THE HEAD AND NOT
THE TAIL, AND YOU WILL ALWAYS BE ON TOP
AND NEVER AT THE BOTTOM. *Deuteronomy 28:13*

Will of God

MY QUESTION *for* GOD

What is God's will for my life?

A MOMENT *with* GOD

Who knows if perhaps you were made queen for just
such a time as this?   ESTHER 4:14

You see me when I travel and when I rest at home.
You know everything I do.   PSALM 139:3

"I know the plans I have for you," says the LORD.
"They are plans for good and not for disaster, to give
you a future and a hope."   JEREMIAH 29:11

Come, let us go up to the mountain of the LORD, to
the house of Jacob's God. There he will teach us his
ways, and we will walk in his paths.   ISAIAH 2:3

Well done, my good and faithful servant. You have
been faithful in handling this small amount, so now
I will give you many more responsibilities.

MATTHEW 25:21

Oh, that we might know the LORD! Let us press on
to know him. He will respond to us.   HOSEA 6:3

So why do you keep calling me "Lord, Lord!" when
you don't do what I say? I will show you what it's like
when someone comes to me, listens to my teaching,
and then follows it.   LUKE 6:46-47

$\mathcal{H}$as there ever been a Christian who has not asked
this question? Sometimes "God's will" seems so vague,
so hard to know. Perhaps the problem is that too often
we're expecting God to reveal something special to us
and we ignore the revelation he's already given in his

Word. The Bible has dozens of clear commands for you to follow: worship only God, love your neighbors and your enemies, use your spiritual gifts, tell the truth, do not covet, do not steal, be sexually pure, remain faithful, don't gossip, be generous, don't take God's name in vain, read his Word regularly, don't let money control you, let the Holy Spirit control your life—the list goes on! Isn't doing all these things God's will for your life? But God also created each person for a specific purpose, and he calls you to do specific tasks. It is usually through steady obedience to God's will, found in his Word, that your specific direction in life can be found. So first make sure you are following God's will in the areas he has already laid out. As you wait for God to reveal what he wants you to do specifically, you should continue to be obedient to the things he calls every person to do. Then, if you happen to miss God's direction for a specific task, you won't have missed God's will for living your everyday life. God is vitally interested in the details of your life, but his primary will for all people is simply obedience.

DIVINE PROMISE

THE LORD SAYS, "I WILL GUIDE YOU ALONG THE BEST PATHWAY FOR YOUR LIFE. I WILL ADVISE YOU AND WATCH OVER YOU." *Psalm 32:8*

Wisdom

MY QUESTION *for* GOD

How do I gain wisdom? How will it help me?

A MOMENT *with* GOD

Fear of the LORD is the foundation of wisdom. Knowledge of the Holy One results in good judgment.   PROVERBS 9:10

Give me an understanding heart so that I can govern your people well and know the difference between right and wrong.   1 KINGS 3:9

My child, don't lose sight of common sense and discernment. Hang on to them, for they will refresh your soul. They are like jewels on a necklace. They keep you safe on your way, and your feet will not stumble. You can go to bed without fear; you will lie down and sleep soundly. . . . For the LORD is your security. He will keep your foot from being caught in a trap.   PROVERBS 3:21-26

Using a dull ax requires great strength, so sharpen the blade. That's the value of wisdom; it helps you succeed.   ECCLESIASTES 10:10

If you need wisdom, ask our generous God, and he will give it to you. He will not rebuke you for asking.

                                                      JAMES 1:5

Solving a complex problem in trigonometry or writing a computer program that will guide a nuclear missile both require great intelligence. But intelligence does not guarantee a balanced, productive, or fulfilling life. On the other hand, success in relationships, witnessing about your faith, and reaching spiritual maturity depend more on wisdom than intelligence. The Bible has so much to say about wisdom (the entire book of Proverbs is devoted to it) because successfully navigating through life requires so much of it. Wisdom helps you recognize that an all-powerful, all-knowing God has designed a moral universe in which there are consequences for your choices, either good or bad. Wisdom begins with understanding your accountability to your Creator and your full dependence on him. It's not *what* you know but *who* you know. Wisdom from God helps you develop a godly perspective that penetrates the deceptive and distorted messages of this world. Wisdom is choosing to apply God's truth and principles to your daily relationships and situations. It helps you know the difference between good and bad, right and wrong.

DIVINE PROMISE

THE WISE ARE MIGHTIER THAN THE STRONG, AND THOSE WITH KNOWLEDGE GROW STRONGER AND STRONGER. *Proverbs 24:5*

Witnessing

How can God use my testimony?

A MOMENT *with* GOD

Moses told his father-in-law everything the LORD had done to Pharaoh and Egypt on behalf of Israel.

EXODUS 18:8

Has the LORD redeemed you? Then speak out! Tell others he has redeemed you from your enemies.

PSALM 107:2

He told them, "Go into all the world and preach the Good News to everyone."   MARK 16:15

God has not given us a spirit of fear and timidity, but of power, love, and self-discipline. So never be ashamed to tell others about our Lord.   2 TIMOTHY 1:7-8

How beautiful are the feet of messengers who bring good news!   ROMANS 10:15

*Y*our friend mentions in casual conversation that she enjoyed a terrific meal at a new restaurant and thinks you would like it too. Someone overhears you and a friend discussing whether or not to see a certain movie and tells you he thought it was great. Both of these people are witnesses. Although the word *witness* brings to mind images of courtrooms or awkward religious proselytizing, to witness simply means to tell about something you have experienced. Everyone who believes in God shares the privilege and responsibility of witnessing. Believing in God isn't about getting into some exclusive group. It's about experiencing something so wonderful that you can't wait to invite others to experience it too. It's about living a life of sharing your divine moments with others. You should always be ready to tell the story of how you came to know and love Jesus. That story is the greatest story you could tell. Who knows? Perhaps sharing your own story will bring a divine moment in someone else's life.

DIVINE PROMISE

THOSE WHO ARE WISE WILL SHINE AS BRIGHT AS THE SKY, AND THOSE WHO LEAD MANY TO RIGHTEOUSNESS WILL SHINE LIKE THE STARS FOREVER.   *Daniel 12:3*

Words

MY QUESTION *for* GOD

How powerful are the words I speak?

A MOMENT *with* GOD

The words of the godly are a life-giving fountain.

PROVERBS 10:11

The words of the godly are like sterling silver.

PROVERBS 10:20

Let everything you say be good and helpful, so that
your words will be an encouragement to those who
hear them.   EPHESIANS 4:29

*O*ur words are like gifts that we give to God or to
other people. The things we say and the meaning behind our words have an enormous impact on those who
hear them. You wouldn't give an obscene gift to the
principal of your school, or even to a friend, and you
certainly wouldn't want to give something insulting to
an enemy. Words are no different. In fact, the greatest
gift you can give to others is not in a box covered with
paper and bows but in the words you use to encourage,
inspire, comfort, and challenge them. Don't let your
words be annoying, insulting, demeaning, or simply
useless. Your words truly matter because what you say
reveals the condition of your heart. Make your words
count so they might become a divine moment in the life
of another person.

DIVINE PROMISE

WISE WORDS ARE MORE VALUABLE THAN
MUCH GOLD AND MANY RUBIES.   *Proverbs 20:15*

Work

MY QUESTION *for* GOD

How do I find meaning in my work?

A Moment *with* God

Make it your goal to live a quiet life, minding your own business and working with your hands, just as we instructed you before. Then people who are not Christians will respect the way you live, and you will not need to depend on others.   1 THESSALONIANS 4:11-12

Whatever you do or say, do it as a representative of the Lord Jesus, giving thanks through him to God the Father.   COLOSSIANS 3:17

You know that these hands of mine have worked to supply my own needs and even the needs of those who were with me. And I have been a constant example of how you can help those in need by working hard.   ACTS 20:34-35

Try to please them all the time, not just when they are watching you. As slaves of Christ, do the will of God with all your heart. Work with enthusiasm, as though you were working for the Lord rather than for people.   EPHESIANS 6:6-7

*W*ork is part of God's plan for our lives, so our work matters to God. Those who work diligently experience many benefits in their own lives and are able to pass them on to others. At its best, work honors God and brings meaning and joy to your life. In your work you should model characteristics of God's work, such as excellence, concern for the well-being of others, purpose, beauty, and service. When you have the perspective that you are actually working for God, you can focus less on the task itself and more on your motives—to help people know God. The excitement and interest that come from having this perspective are not primarily from your work but from the One for whom you work. God promises two basic rewards for faithful work, regardless of the job: You are a more credible witness to unbelievers, and your needs are met without having to depend on others financially. Whatever your job, there is immense dignity in all honest human labor because your work is an opportunity to serve God and others. Believe that God has placed you in your position for a reason, and then do your work well until he opens a door of opportunity for you to move on.

DIVINE PROMISE

WORK WILLINGLY AT WHATEVER YOU DO, AS THOUGH YOU WERE WORKING FOR THE LORD RATHER THAN FOR PEOPLE. REMEMBER THAT THE LORD WILL GIVE YOU AN INHERITANCE AS YOUR REWARD, AND THAT THE MASTER YOU ARE SERVING IS CHRIST.   *Colossians 3:23-24*

Worry

MY QUESTION *for* GOD
How can I stop worrying about everything?

A Moment *with* God

Don't worry about tomorrow, for tomorrow will bring its own worries. Today's trouble is enough for today.

MATTHEW 6:34

Here on earth you will have many trials and sorrows. But take heart, because I have overcome the world.

JOHN 16:33

*Y*ou can trust God to take care of you because he is faithful. He loves you and promises to guide you to a perfect, eternal future if you follow him. Jesus never promised a problem-free life; in fact, he guaranteed that life would not be easy. So don't be surprised by hard times, and don't be afraid of them. There is no problem that Jesus can't handle or overcome. Most of the things you worry about might never happen anyway, so don't waste time on "what ifs," either about your past or your future. Turn your worry time into prayer time.

Divine Promise

THE LORD KEEPS WATCH OVER YOU AS YOU COME AND GO, BOTH NOW AND FOREVER.
Psalm 121:8

Worry

MY QUESTION *for* GOD

Where can I turn when I start to get overwhelmed by worry?

A MOMENT *with* GOD

That is why I tell you not to worry about everyday life—whether you have enough food and drink, or enough clothes to wear. Isn't life more than food, and your body more than clothing? Look at the birds. They don't plant or harvest or store food in barns, for your heavenly Father feeds them. And aren't you far more valuable to him than they are? Can all your worries add a single moment to your life?

MATTHEW 6:25-27

Worry is a natural part of life, but too much of it can distract and paralyze you. It crowds out the good in your life and keeps you focused on your problems, which only makes them seem worse. The more you worry, the more overwhelmed you will feel. Worry becomes sinful when it prevents you from thinking about anything else, including God. The Bible teaches that you find rest from worry when you admit that you can't control the future, and then you entrust yourself—and your loved ones—to the God who does. As you release your concerns to God, you will find your troubles getting smaller and smaller. When you entrust your cares to God instead of worrying about them, you will find yourself overjoyed rather than overwhelmed.

Divine Promise

GOD IS OUR REFUGE AND STRENGTH, ALWAYS
READY TO HELP IN TIMES OF TROUBLE.   *Psalm 46:1*

Worship

My Question *for* God

How do I worship God?

A Moment *with* God

Then David praised the Lord in the presence of the
whole assembly: "O Lord, the God of our ancestor
Israel, may you be praised forever and ever! Yours,
O Lord, is the greatness, the power, the glory, the
victory, and the majesty. Everything in the heavens
and on earth is yours, O Lord, and this is your
kingdom. We adore you as the one who is over all
things. Wealth and honor come from you alone, for
you rule over everything. Power and might are in
your hand, and at your discretion people are made
great and given strength. O our God, we thank you
and praise your glorious name!"   1 Chronicles 29:10-13

Oh, how great are God's riches and wisdom and
knowledge! How impossible it is for us to understand
his decisions and his ways! For who can know the
Lord's thoughts? Who knows enough to give him
advice? And who has given him so much that he needs
to pay it back? For everything comes from him and

exists by his power and is intended for his glory. All glory to him forever! Amen.   ROMANS 11:33-36

We do not think of our world as a worshiping culture, let alone an idolatrous culture, but our behavior suggests otherwise. Consider our weekly gatherings of thousands of frenzied fans observing a ceremony of men dressed in strange garb acting out a violent drama of conquest. Others stay at home and join in by way of a small glowing shrine set up in the family room. Or consider the way thousands of young people scream and throw themselves at the stage where their rock-star idols are performing. Fans of professional football or celebrity singers are probably not even aware that their behavior could be described as worship. Human beings were created to worship. To worship is to ascribe ultimate value to an object, person, or God, and then to revere, adore, pay homage to, and obey by ordering the priorities of our lives around whatever it is we worship. The Bible teaches that God alone is worthy of our worship. True worship, then, is the recognition of who God is and of who you are in relation to him. Ultimately, everything you do should be based on what you think of the almighty God and how you worship him. If you aren't giving honor to God, then you are worshiping someone or something else. More than anything else, true worship connects you with God, your only source of lasting hope and joy.

DIVINE PROMISE

THEREFORE, GOD ELEVATED HIM TO THE PLACE
OF HIGHEST HONOR AND GAVE HIM THE NAME
ABOVE ALL OTHER NAMES, THAT AT THE NAME
OF JESUS EVERY KNEE SHOULD BOW, IN HEAVEN
AND ON EARTH AND UNDER THE EARTH, AND
EVERY TONGUE CONFESS THAT JESUS CHRIST IS
LORD, TO THE GLORY OF GOD THE FATHER.

Philippians 2:9-11

Worth

MY QUESTIONS *for* GOD

What is my worth? Am I valuable to God?

A MOMENT *with* GOD

God created human beings in his own image. In the
image of God he created them; male and female he
created them.   GENESIS 1:27

You made [people] only a little lower than God and
crowned them with glory and honor.   PSALM 8:5

The LORD has declared today that you are his people,
his own special treasure, just as he promised, and that
you must obey all his commands.   DEUTERONOMY 26:18

Even before he made the world, God loved us and
chose us in Christ to be holy and without fault in his
eyes. God decided in advance to adopt us into his
own family by bringing us to himself through Jesus
Christ. This is what he wanted to do, and it gave him

great pleasure. So we praise God for the glorious grace he has poured out on us who belong to his dear Son. He is so rich in kindness and grace that he purchased our freedom with the blood of his Son and forgave our sins.   EPHESIANS 1:4-7

*D*o you get your sense of self-worth from a combination of looks, accomplishments, grades, possessions, and social status? This is a precarious way to live. If you have a bad hair day or get sick, if your next performance doesn't exceed your last, if you let your grades slip, if you lose your favorite electronic gadget, or if your friends are shallow and fickle—then you also lose your sense of self-worth. The most secure and lasting place to find worth is in your relationship with God. It is truly a divine moment when you realize just how much God values you! God created you and knew you intimately before you were born. He loved you enough to rescue you from eternal punishment for your sins through Jesus' death and resurrection. Because of this, you know you have tremendous value and worth in God's eyes. Because of the magnitude of God's forgiveness and grace and his love for you, he is worthy of your praise, gratitude, and love in return.

DIVINE PROMISE

HOW PRECIOUS ARE YOUR THOUGHTS ABOUT ME, O GOD.   *Psalm 139:17*

Index

ABILITIES 1
ABSOLUTES 2
ACCEPTANCE 4
ACCOMPLISHMENTS 5
ACCOUNTABILITY 6
ADDICTION 8
ADVICE 11
ANGER 13
ANTICIPATION 14
APATHY 16
APOLOGY 18
APPEARANCE 20
APPROVAL 21
ARTS 23
ASHAMED 25
AWESOME 26
BALANCE 28
BEGINNINGS 29
BELONGING 31
BEST 32
BIBLE 34
BOREDOM 36
BROKENNESS 37
BURNOUT 39
BUSYNESS 40
CALL OF GOD 42
CHALLENGES 43
CHANGE 46
CHARACTER 48
CHOICES 49, 51, 52
CHURCH 53
COMMITMENT 55
COMMUNICATION 57
COMPETITION 59
COMPROMISE 61
CONSCIENCE 63
CONSEQUENCES 64

CONTENTMENT 66
CONVERSATION 67
CONVICTIONS 69
COURAGE 71
CREATIVITY 72
CRISIS 73
CULTURE 75
DANGER 76
DECISIONS 78
DEMANDS 79
DESIRES 80, 82
DETERMINATION 83
DISAPPROVAL 85
DISCOURAGEMENT 86
DOUBT 88
EMOTIONS 89
EMPTINESS 91
ENCOURAGEMENT 92
ENDURANCE 94
ENEMIES 96
ENERGY 97
ETERNITY 98
EVIL 101
EXAMPLE 102
EXCELLENCE 104
EXPERIENCE 105
FAILURE 106
FAITH 108
FEAR 109
FEELINGS 111
FINISHING 112
FLEXIBILITY 114
FORGIVENESS 116
FREEDOM 118
FRIENDSHIP 119
FUN 120
FUTURE 122

GOALS   123
GOSSIP   125
GRACE   126
GUARDING YOUR
    HEART   127
GUIDANCE   129
HABITS   130
HAND OF GOD   132
HARD-HEARTEDNESS   134
HEALTH   136
HEAVEN   137
HELP   138
HOLY SPIRIT   139
HONESTY   141
HOPE   143
HUMILITY   144
HURTS   145
IMPACT   147
IMPOSSIBLE   148
INFLUENCE   150
INSECURITY   152
INSIGNIFICANCE   153
INTEGRITY   154
INVITATION   156
INVOLVEMENT   157
JOY   159
JUDGING OTHERS   160
KNOWLEDGE AND
    LEARNING   161
LIMITATIONS   163
LISTENING   165, 166
LONELINESS   167
LOVE   168, 170
MEANING   171
MEMORIES   173
MERCY   174
MIRACLES   176
MISTAKES   177
MOTIVATION   179

MUSIC   181
MYSTERY   183
NATURE   184
OBEDIENCE   186
OPPORTUNITIES   188
OVERWHELMED   189
PAIN   191
PANIC   192
PASSION   194
PAST   196
PATIENCE   198
PEACE   200
PERFECTION   201
PERSECUTION   202
PERSPECTIVE   203, 205
PLANS   206
PLEASURE   208
POTENTIAL   209
POWER OF GOD   211
PRAYER   213, 214
PRESSURE   216
PRIORITIES   217
PROMISES OF GOD   219, 220
PURPOSE   222, 224
QUESTIONS   225
QUIET TIME   227
REGRETS   230
RELATIONSHIPS   232
RELEVANCE   234
REPENTANCE   236
REPUTATION   237
RESPECT   238
RESPONSIBILITY   240
REST   241
REWARDS   243
RISKS   244
ROMANCE   246
SACRIFICE   247
SALVATION   249

Satisfaction 251
Seeking God 253
Self-Control 255
Serving 257
Sharing 258
Sin 260
Sorrow 262
Spiritual Dryness 263
Spiritual Gifts 265
Spiritual Warfare 267
Strengths and
    Weaknesses 269
Stress 270
Stubbornness 272
Success 274
Suffering 275, 277
Supernatural 279
Surprise 280
Temptation 282, 284
Testing 285

Thankfulness 287
Thoughts 288
Time 290
Timing of God 291
Trust 293
Truth 294
Unity 297
Usefulness 298
Values 300
Victory 302
Vulnerability 304
Warnings 306
Will of God 307
Wisdom 310
Witnessing 312
Words 313
Work 314
Worry 316, 318
Worship 319
Worth 321

DIVINE
MOMENTS
Books